AFRICAN ISLANDS
in style

AFRICAN ISLANDS
in style

DAVID ROGERS
JEREMY JOWELL
IAN JOHNSON

AFRICA
Geographic

contents

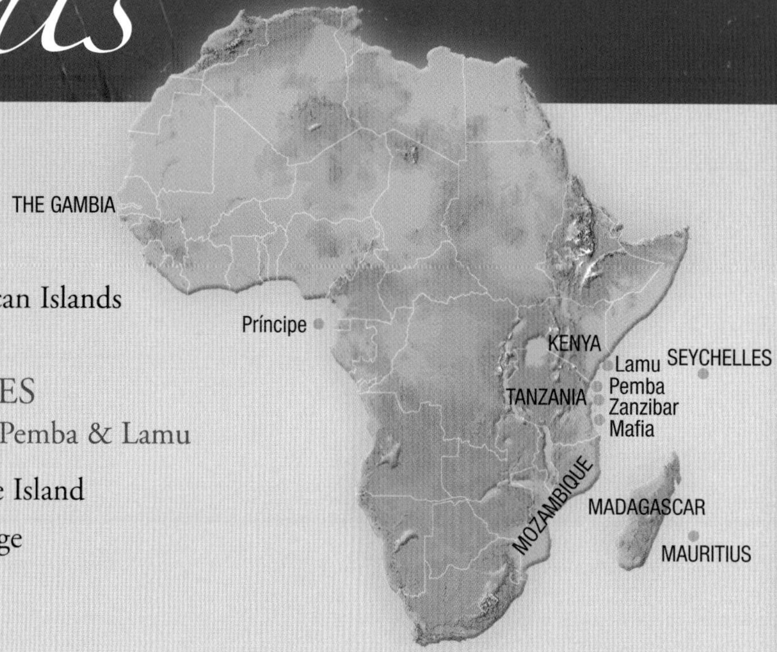

THE GAMBIA

Príncipe

KENYA
SEYCHELLES
Lamu
TANZANIA
Pemba
Zanzibar
Mafia

MOZAMBIQUE
MADAGASCAR
MAURITIUS

introducing
african islands

The tropical islands that lie scattered across the western Indian Ocean have had a colourful and turbulent history. Their ports have seen the arrival of pirates, Arab traders, slave runners and colonising European powers. Today, however, turbulence is a thing of the past, and the islands typify the laid-back life. All that remains of those forceful invaders are weathered forts, decaying colonial mansions and people who speak languages that bear echoes of their visitors of long ago.

The true beauty of these exotic islands lies in their smiling and friendly people, their scenery, which ranges from towering sand dunes and sandy, palm-lined beaches to exuberant greenery, and, above all, the multicoloured underwater wonderland that surrounds them. These attractions draw tourists from all over the world, who come to escape the city hubbub and to experience for themselves these serene slices of paradise and the splendid retreats that have sprung up on their shores.

This beautiful book, *African Islands in Style*, explores some of these island destinations. The travel experts at Africa Geographic, in collaboration with our experienced journalists and photographers, have put together a selection of lodges, resorts and retreats that will send you hunting for your passport. We visit magical Madagascar, with its fascinating endemic wildlife and unique scenery; Mauritius, the favourite of honeymooners and the world-weary; and the Seychelles, not called the 'Garden of Eden' for nothing. We also explore Mozambique, with its fascinating Bazaruto and Quirimbas archipelagos; Tanzania, home of spice-fragranced Zanzibar, forested Pemba and the coral reef sanctuary of Mafia Island; and the mysterious island of Lamu, off the coast of Kenya. Some of the accommodation options we feature provide pampered luxury, and offer everything the sophisticated tourist desires. Others are situated on wilder, private islands, or in reserve areas, where the number of visitors is limited to ensure privacy and a low-impact footprint on the environment, but the service is still five-star. The choice is yours.

We also cross the continent to investigate two new destinations in steamy West Africa – we showcase a beautiful resort in the fantasy island republic of São Tomé and Príncipe, and visit a luxury eco-lodge near the mouth of the Gambia River.

Hopefully, this evocatively written and photographed *African Islands in Style* will encourage you to pack your bags and to experience for yourself the continent's finest island getaways.

ANDREW WOODBURN

A dhow slices through the ocean.
CHARLES GRIEVES-COOK

Strung along the coast of East Africa are islands that offer a cornucopia of contrasts. Tanzania's Mafia Island is an exquisite, unspoilt reserve; Zanzibar brims with smiles, history and natural beauty, and Pemba lies quietly beneath its cloak of dense, lush vegetation. To the north is Kenya's serene and alluring Lamu Island. The island lodges are irresistible – some are rustically charming; others have an exotic, luxurious appeal.

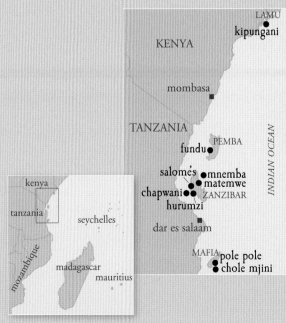

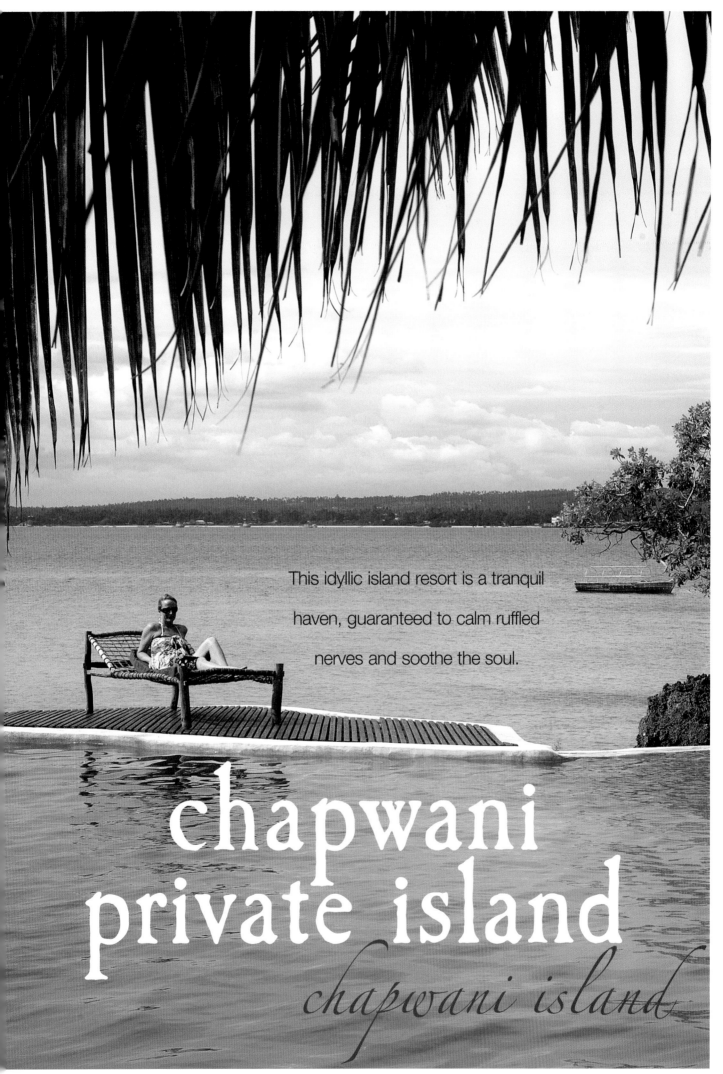

This idyllic island resort is a tranquil haven, guaranteed to calm ruffled nerves and soothe the soul.

chapwani private island

chapwani island

'If you need to relax, then you've come to the right place'

PREVIOUS SPREAD Chapwani Island rises from a dusk-tinted sea.

There's plenty of time to soak up the sun on the pool deck.

THIS SPREAD The guest areas are open-sided and convivial.

Schools of dolphins patrol the region.

Chapwani Island – home to numerous bird species, dik-dik and a restful lodge.

The thatched bungalows are private and tranquil.

The wooden four-poster beds are swathed in netting.

Another hot day dawns in Zanzibar and I leave the Stone Town hustle for some quiet time on Chapwani Private Island, west of Zanzibar. A small boat with an orange canopy putters up to the beach. The skipper loads my luggage and we motor out across the bay. 'It's about four kilometres to the island and will take us 30 minutes,' he says, steering the boat over the gentle Indian Ocean swells.

As I step ashore, I'm met by Ali Hemed, the island manager. 'Welcome to Chapwani. We are a small island; you can walk the entire length in 15 minutes. There are many interesting things here, including thousands of fruit bats that fly off the trees at dusk. If you need to relax, then you've come to the right place.'

Chapwani is also home to a herd of dik-dik and numerous birds, including the African paradise-flycatcher, whimbrels, egrets, plovers and pied kingfishers. There are palm trees and baobabs, small coves, sandy beaches and coral reefs.

Accommodation is in five thatched-roof bungalows, each containing two separate en-suite units. The rooms are simply, yet comfortably furnished, with wooden four-poster beds, mosquito nets, ceiling fans and a traditional Zanzibari writing desk. A woven banana-leaf blind at the window lets in the cooling sea breeze.

The island is excellent for swimming, snorkelling and canoeing. It's a perfect base for exploring Zanzibar, and excursions such as spice tours and swimming with dolphins can be organised.

After settling in, I stroll along the path that winds across the centre of the island. Startled, a shy dik-dik crashes away into the bushes. Further on I hear excited squeaks coming from the trees. Beating through the dense undergrowth, I come face to face with a huge colony of fruit bats hanging upside in the branches. They squawk noisily and fly off.

Also known as Grave Island, Chapwani has a naval burial yard dating to the 1840s, when the British Royal Navy played an active role in stamping out the East African slave trade that operated out of Zanzibar. Many seamen died, some from disease and drowning, others from accidents and skirmishes with slave owners. The graveyard is also the resting place of 24 sailors from the British *HMS Pegasus*, which was attacked by a German cruiser during World War I.

After a post-lunch snooze, I wake as the late afternoon sun begins to drop through thick clouds, casting shafts of orange light onto the ocean. I walk along the north-western shore, where the tide has receded to reveal shallow pools rippled with red reflections. Flocks of birds flash across the sky; in the distance, dhows are silhouetted against faraway islands.

Chapwani's restaurant offers a blend of Oriental, African and European cuisine with the emphasis, naturally, on fresh seafood. I tuck into calamari salad, followed by papaya soup, then tasty red snapper served with grilled vegetables and spicy pilau rice. After dinner I walk along the beach, watching the stars above and the lights of Stone Town twinkling across the bay. Sleep comes easily, accompanied by the soporific sound of the ocean.

details

When to go
Chapwani Private Island is closed during April and May, the wettest months of the year. February and March are good months to view the fruit bats as there are no leaves on the trees.

How to get there
The island is four kilometres from Zanzibar. Transfers from the airport can be pre-arranged with tour operators. Alternatively, contact Chapwani Private Island directly and its boat will collect you from the beach in front of Livingstone Restaurant, next to Tembo Hotel.

Who to contact
Tel. (+255-77) 743 3102, e-mail *chapwani@zitec.org*

chole mjini
lodge

chole island

A tropical hideaway with treetop accommodation, silky turquoise

waters, abundant marine life and a responsible approach to tourism –

Chole Mjini Lodge is a unique paradise.

Ever since I was young, I've always wanted to sleep in a wooden treehouse, high up in the branches. Unfortunately, my forest fantasy was never fulfilled. Now, here on Tanzania's tiny Chole Island, my dream is about to be realised. But this is no ramshackle dwelling knocked together with a few planks and a handful of nails. This is Chole Mjini, a unique island lodge whose seven treehouse chalets offer a lofty luxury adventure.

Owned and operated by Jean and Anne de Villiers, Chole Mjini's open-sided treetop units, created by local craftsmen using local materials, are mostly built around baobab trees and feature four-poster beds with Egyptian cotton sheets. Each treehouse has a sundeck, while the bathroom and shower are situated on ground level. There is no electricity on Chole, and the lodge is justifiably proud of its minimal carbon footprint. Lighting is provided by kerosene lamps, but you can still charge your batteries, and enjoy a hot shower or a chilled drink, thanks to solar and wind power and innovative design.

Chole Island is a short dhow ride from Mafia Island and lies at the heart of the Mafia Island Marine Park. The island, just one kilometre in length, is home to numerous ancient ruins; Popo Park, the world's first sanctuary for fruit bats; and a traditional village where life has changed little over the centuries.

Jean, a biologist by profession, is a passionate scuba diver. 'When we first visited Chole, the local authorities tried to interest us in land they had allocated for a hotel. Initially, we feared the impact such a project would have on the environment, but sensitive development has made it a great success, despite our original reservations.'

The lodge has played a huge role in building a better future for the people of Chole. For every guest, US$10 per night is used to assist ongoing community projects. Chole Mjini has helped to build and run a kindergarten, classrooms, houses for teachers and a small hospital, and contributes to the secondary education of some 90 students.

The cuisine at the lodge comprises mainly freshly caught seafood, which is often prepared in traditional Swahili style. One night, tables are laid in an old ruin entangled in the roots of a huge fig tree, its branches festooned with hurricane lanterns. The avocado soup is superb; so is the red snapper in coconut batter with rice, spicy salsa and roasted red pepper that follow.

The next morning I go snorkelling to the rocky outcrop of Kirongo. With unspoilt reefs and over 400 species of fish, the underwater world in the marine park is spectacular. I dive down, clicking away at the dottybacks, bannerfish, damsels and multicoloured wrasse. Later, I take a trip to nearby Juani Island. As the light softens, I walk around the old Shirazi Persian ruins, dating back to the 12th century. We coast down the channel, admiring the birdlife perched in the mangroves. A big red sun sinks behind Mafia Island and I crack open a cold Kilimanjaro beer as we sail back across Chole Bay.

PREVIOUS SPREAD A dining table is set in ruins that have been overgrown by the roots of a wild fig tree.

Dhows have plied these waters for hundreds of years.

THIS SPREAD Hidden in the tree canopy, the wooden chalets offer panoramic views and complete privacy.

Chole Island is a short dhow ride from Mafia Island.

Meals are generally served in the thatched dining/sitting room.

A treehouse with a difference.

Luxurious furnishings and fine views.

*Ever since I was young,
I've always wanted to sleep
in a wooden treehouse…*

details

When to go
The resort is open all year. The weather is most comfortable from July to late December. Scuba diving is best from October to March.

How to get there
Chole Island is reached via Mafia Island. There is a daily flight from Dar es Salaam to Mafia. Chole Mjini Lodge will send a car to fetch guests from the airstrip and transfer them to the boat terminal for the five-minute ride to the island.

Who to contact
Tel. (+255-784) 52 0799, or e-mail *2chole@bushmail.net* or *cholemjini@intotanzania.com*

fundu lagoon

pemba island

It's impossible not to fall in love with Fundu Lagoon and its

irresistible combination of laid-back chic, sublime views and an

underwater wonderland that is unequalled anywhere on earth.

It's another beautiful blue-sky day on Pemba Island as our speedboat cruises smoothly over the aquamarine ocean. We've just left Fundu Lagoon en route to Misali Island, one of the best snorkelling spots in the Zanzibar archipelago. The scuba divers kit up and flop overboard. I don my snorkelling gear and follow them into a magic world of coral-nibbling parrotfish, darting schools of small silver fish and pairs of graceful yellow butterflyfish.

Situated on the Pemba Island's Wambaa Peninsula, Fundu Lagoon is one of the prime beach lodges in Tanzania. To reach it, we drive past plantations of fruit and cloves to Mkoani port, where a boat is to ferry me to the resort.

Fundu Lagoon manager Matt Semark and his wife Anie arrived recently from running a resort in Indonesia. 'The major attraction here is the underwater world. When I first dived these reefs, I was amazed at the quality of coral and quantity of fish.'

The resort has a certificated, well-equipped dive centre with five instructors and, as expected, there is no shortage of water-based activities. Apart from snorkelling and scuba diving, there are sunset dhow cruises, deep-sea fishing trips, canoeing and catamaran charters. Early-morning dolphin safaris almost always reveal large schools of spinner dolphins near Misali Island. There are also excursions to local villages, spice tours and a trip to Ngezi Forest Reserve to see vervet monkeys and the local fruit bat, the Pemba flying fox.

Fundu Lagoon is the epitome of rustic chic. Its 16 stylish tented suites are linked by sandy

I don my snorkelling gear and follow them into a magic world

walkways to the reception and dining areas. Each has a large sundeck with recliner chairs. The resort also has a games room, satellite television and a sophisticated spa. The restaurant changes its menu daily, with a highlight being the Sunday Swahili evening. Honeymooners and romantics can enjoy candlelit dinners on the beach.

I motor out to Misali Island with a group of scuba enthusiasts. After their initial dive, we go ashore for a picnic lunch. The island was declared a protected conservation area in 1998 and no fishing is allowed. 'Many green and hawksbill turtles nest on our beaches, but we don't put markers to indicate the sites because fishermen may come and remove the eggs,' says ranger Abas Hamadi Othman.

After lunch, while the rest of the group motor off for a second dive, I stay behind to snorkel the shallow reef. An hour later they return with broad smiles. 'What a dive! We saw loads of fish,' says a British tourist. 'But what will make you really jealous is that a huge school of spinner dolphins spent 15 minutes leaping and playing right next to the boat!'

I am green with envy. I guess I'll just have to return to Fundu Lagoon sometime soon.

PREVIOUS SPREAD Enchanting wooden walkways link the various facilities at Fundu Lagoon.

THIS SPREAD From the private verandas, guests never tire of the ever-changing patterns of light on the water.

Take a sunset cruise on a dhow.

Fundu Lagoon's underwater world is spectacular, and is much beloved by the resort's owners.

The resort's pool lies at the edge of the ocean.

The suites epitomise rustic chic, with their locally hewn furniture and sumptuous bedlinen and drapes.

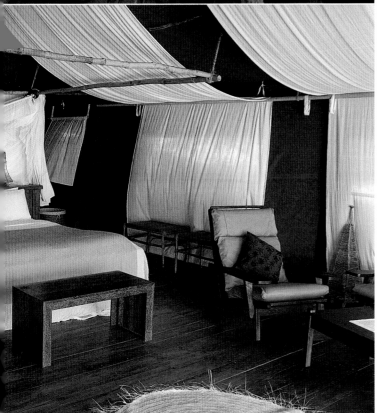

details

When to go
Fundu Lagoon is closed from mid-April to mid-June. The best months for diving are from October to March. December and January can be very hot and humid.

How to get there
You can fly in from either Dar es Salaam or Zanzibar, or take a ferry to Mkoani port. On arrival, Fundu staff will transport you by road and boat to the resort.

Who to contact
Tel. (+255-75) 478 9994, e-mail *reservations@fundulagoon.com* or go to *www.fundulagoon.com*

236 hurumzi
zanzibar island

Once the home of a wealthy Indian trader, 236 Hurumzi has been resplendently restored. Guests here will feel like potentates as they leave its doors to explore the sights and sounds of historical Stone Town.

The Crystal Room ... has high wooden ceilings, ornate chandeliers, carved doors and hand-painted windowpanes

ANDREW WOODBURN

I emerge from the warm, spice-fragranced air into the calm of the hotel foyer. There aren't many places in the world where one can stay in a historic monument in a World Heritage Site, I muse as I check into 236 Hurumzi, one of the top hotels in Stone Town, Zanzibar.

The building has a fascinating history. It was erected in the early 1800s by Tharia Topan, a powerful Indian merchant, who was permitted by the Sultan of Zanzibar to build the second highest home in Stone Town after his own ceremonial palace, the House of Wonders. Later, it was in this building that British authorities paid Arab slave owners to free their slaves, and the name 'Hurumzi' is derived from the Swahili words, *uhuru mzee*, which means 'free the men'.

In 1991, Thomas Green began to acquire the edifice, by lease and by purchase, and started to restore it. 'We have attempted to create a special atmosphere, where each room is unique and its character determined by beautiful artefacts.' Formerly known as the Emerson & Green, after Green and former partner Emerson Skeens, 236 Hurumzi has 16 suites. Each is beautifully decorated with Persian, Indian and Arab elements, and is equipped with large stone bathtubs and Zanzibari beds. Mine is called the Crystal Room – it has high wooden ceilings, ornate chandeliers, carved doors and hand-painted windowpanes.

I stroll down to the Forodhani Gardens where I'm greeted by warm smiles from the vendors who cajole me into tasting their food. 'Here are tiger prawns, shrimps, tuna, blue marlin, calamari and kingfish kebabs. There's also lobster and big crabs. Everything you see is fresh,' says one trader, indicating his seafood spread. I opt for tuna and marlin kebabs, which are delicious, and wash them down with a glass of sweet sugar-cane juice, manually squeezed in an archaic machine.

The next morning I set off to explore the town's winding alleyways. Within minutes I'm hopelessly lost, but that's the magic of this meandering maze – you're never quite sure where you are and every corner brings another surprise. Crumbling yellow buildings with broken balconies rise above the narrow streets. Black-veiled Muslim women fry balls of dough. Children sit in a darkened classroom, reciting verses from the Koran. In the fish market, piles of small silver snappers are displayed symmetrically on bloody concrete slabs.

I dine at 236 Hurumzi's famous rooftop Tower Top Restaurant, with its panoramic views over the minarets and church spires of Stone Town. I leave my shoes at the door and take a seat, Arabian-style, on cushions and carpets. Accompanied by music and dancers, my five-course dinner arrives. Lentil curry puffs are followed by pumpkin-coconut soup, then king prawns with cinnamon rice and baked cauliflower, and tandoori chicken with potatoes in coconut sauce. Dessert is tiramisu and a tangy lemon tart.

The following evening, I stroll to the waterfront to watch the sunset. White-sailed dhows drift by as the muezzin summons people to their prayers. All is peaceful in Stone Town as another sultry day in Zanzibar comes to an end.

PREVIOUS SPREAD A bedroom to inspire dreams of Persian princes and magical genies.

A walk through the alleys of Stone Town will reveal friendly children and beautiful, ornately carved Zanzibari doors.

THIS SPREAD Zanzibar Island spills into the warm Indian Ocean.

The furnishings at 236 Hurumzi reflect the splendour of its history.

Breakfast at the rooftop Tower Top Restaurant.

Vibrant local art can be purchased at Stone Town's market.

Pulsating music and lively dancers entertain the guests.

details

When to go
Weather conditions throughout the year are generally good, although it can be hot and humid from February to May. The hotel is closed in May for annual refurbishment.

How to get there
Visitors arriving at Tanzania's Dar es Salaam international airport can reach Zanzibar via regional airlines, charter flights or boat. Taxis can be taken to Stone Town. The hotel is situated in Hurumzi Street, near the Forodhani Gardens.

Who to contact
Tel. (+255-77) 742 3266, e-mail *236hurumzibookings@zanlink. com* or *anything@236hurumzi.com*, or go to *www.236hurumzi.com*

kipungani
explorer
lamu island

Perched on the southern tip of

legendary Lamu Island, Kipungani

Explorer is a dream hideaway for those

who just want to get away from it all...

It comes as no surprise that a significant – and growing – proportion of Kipungani's guests are newlywed couples. Overlooking the tranquil waters of the sheltered Kipungani Channel, on the edge of a near-deserted 12-kilometre white beach, this has to be one of the most tranquil and romantic settings on the entire African coast.

I arrived at Kipungani the only way you can: by speedboat from Lamu airport. Stepping ashore onto a sponge-soft sandbar, I was handed a delicious juice cocktail and a damp towel, and I immediately felt like I was on honeymoon myself. The resort is a calming combination of the luxurious and the laid-back: simple thatch and palm-mat bandas furnished with soft king-sized beds, hanging cushion-piled 'moon beds' (hammocks), and lavish personal toiletries – inspiring a correspondent from UK's *The Guardian* to describe the bandas as 'some of the most glamorous beach huts in the world'.

Here, guests can enjoy simple pleasures like fishing and lazing by the pool, or go kayaking and snorkelling. The cuisine is highly regarded for its delicious seafood dishes. But for me, Kipungani's real crowning glory is its staff, whose kind reception and friendly attention to detail are unsurpassed.

For me, Kipungani's real crowning glory is its staff, whose kind reception and friendly attention to detail are unsurpassed

For a destination that is trying to perfect one of the gentlest-treading ecotourism experiences in Africa, however, Kipungani has its sights set on an altogether more modest kind of accolade. And, when talking to the 300 residents of Kipungani village, you get the impression that this little eco-lodge is truly succeeding in bringing the benefits of tourism to those who most need them. As well as employing a majority of its staff from Kipungani and nearby Mpeketoni, the lodge buys all its seafood from local fishermen, repairs its seven boats in their boatyards, and hires local craftsmen to weave the makuti thatch and makeka palm leaves from which its bandas are constructed. Most guests make a specific point of visiting the village – a 15-minute walk through sun-dappled mangroves – where the lodge has helped to build a thriving primary school, and where it recently opened the village's first permanent health clinic. The clinic is staffed by a local nurse, Nafisa Mohamed, whose salary is paid by Kipungani's owners, Heritage Hotels.

Kipungani has recently taken on the services of a full-time cultural guide, who takes visitors on day trips to the bustling markets and memorable maritime museum of Lamu's Stone Town, as well as the evocative ruins of the 14th-century fort on neighbouring Manda Island. More energetic visitors can go kayaking in the Lamu Channel, take coast-hugging voyages aboard Kipungani's 10-metre dhow, or rub shoulders with 'Africa's most fearless dolphins' on snorkelling trips to the nearby Kinyika Rocks.

For most visitors, though, one of the greatest pleasures here is going to sleep with your screen door open to the elements, looking out over a sea shimmering with millions of reflected stars.

PREVIOUS SPREAD Smiling service, fine food and tropical splendour – Kipungani Explorer has it all.

The setting sun descends behind approaching storm clouds.

THIS SPREAD The bandas are rustic in appearance, belying their comfortable interiors.

Relaxing on the beach – in Kipungani style.

The Lamu Channel can be explored on a dhow.

Views from the bandas reveal tropical vegetation and sapphire-blue water.

The lodge supports local fishermen by buying their catches.

TEXT BY RALPH JOHNSTONE

details

When to go
The lodge is open all year. Conditions are hot and humid.

How to get there
The main airport for Lamu is on Manda Island, from where a boat transfer for guests is arranged by the lodge.

Who to contact
Heritage Hotels, tel. (+254-20) 71 6628, e-mail *sales@heritagehotels.co.ke* or go to *www.heritage-eastafrica.com*

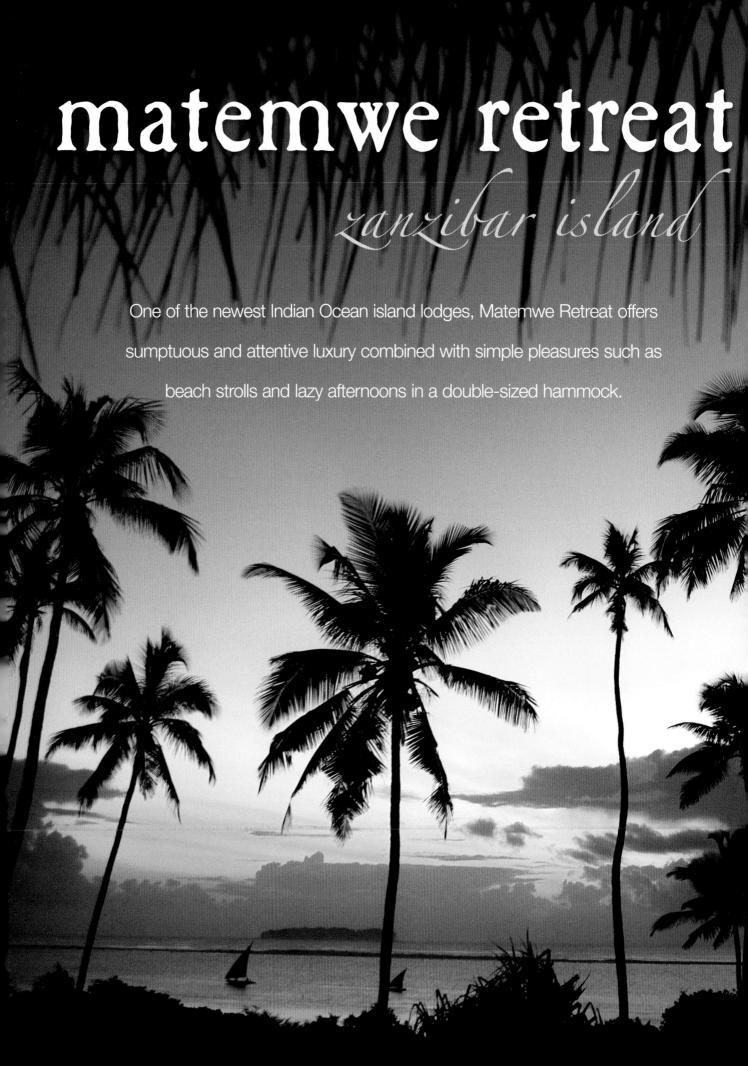

matemwe retreat

zanzibar island

One of the newest Indian Ocean island lodges, Matemwe Retreat offers

sumptuous and attentive luxury combined with simple pleasures such as

beach strolls and lazy afternoons in a double-sized hammock.

1 **Leaving Stone Town,** we drive northwards across Zanzibar Island. We cruise through corridors of coconut palms, pass lush green fields and small rural villages. Colourfully dressed women sell fruit and vegetables on the side of the road. We pass men pedalling bicycles overladen with bundles of wood, sugar cane or baskets of oranges. Carefree children chase chickens across the street. For the last few kilometres we bounce along a dust track, through the sprawling village of Matemwe where several games of soccer are in progress.

Our destination is Matemwe Retreat, on the island's north-east coast. This romantic getaway opened in January 2007 and, with just three ultra-luxurious suites, it is setting new standards in Zanzibar. The lodge's manager, Nigel Folker, shows me around. 'Most of our visitors just want to relax and enjoy the seclusion of our wonderful villas, but there's a lot more to experience here. We offer snorkelling and scuba trips to Mnemba Atoll, the best underwater spot around the island, and also conduct fishing outings, reef walks at low tide and guided village tours.'

With panoramic views through the palm trees to turquoise waters, the split-level villas are spectacular. Made from local materials, the ground floor features a spacious bedroom and en-suite bathroom with a romantic bathtub overlooking the Indian Ocean. The bedroom leads on to a wooden veranda with a double hammock, cocktail bar and lounge area. The upper level is an intimate rooftop terrace with couches, tanning deck and a plunge pool. Each villa is serviced by a personal butler.

Matemwe Retreat and its nearby main lodge, Matemwe Bungalows, have a sincere interest in the local community. They employ workers from the village and have assisted the locals to acquire fresh water and electricity. In addition, they have helped to fund classrooms and sponsor the education of several promising students.

Next morning I wake before sunrise and stroll down to the village. The women are already hard at work, wading through the shallows to collect seaweed which will be dried and used to produce cosmetics and medicine. The sky lightens and I walk along, chatting to the children. One man brushes his teeth and the fishermen prepare their boats for a day on the ocean.

Later, I join a snorkelling expedition to Mnemba Atoll and we cruise out over the clear blue water. After kitting up, I drop into Zanzibar's underwater world. Thousands of fish flit around the coral. Butterflyfish, parrotfish, angelfish and a school of goldbar wrasse. I also dive down for a close look at a blue starfish spreadeagled on the bottom.

After lunch and a siesta in the hammock, I spend the afternoon chilling out on the rooftop terrace. The sun sets and Paul, my butler, brings dinner to my villa. I tuck into lobster tail with mango segments, followed by fried lamb, crispy potatoes and vegetables. Relaxed and replete, I sit outside and savour the sounds of the island. A gentle wind rustles the palm fronds, insects chirp and waves crash on the distant reef. Like giant fireflies, paraffin lamps on fishing boats flicker across the ocean.

PREVIOUS SPREAD Sometimes it's so quiet at Matemwe that all you can hear is the rustle of the palm leaves in the breeze.

THIS SPREAD The upper level of each villa has couches, a tanning deck and a plunge pool.

Matemwe and its beach are popular with honeymooners.

Paradise is framed by a bathroom window.

Matemwe, opened in January 2007, has just three suites.

The bed are king-sized, the soft furnishings sensual and the views sublime.

*Relaxed and replete,
I sit outside and savour
the sounds of the island*

details

When to go
Matemwe Retreat is closed for the rainy season during April and May. Weather during the rest of the year is generally fine. Whales visit this coast between August and October.

How to get there
The fight from Dar es Salaam to Stone Town in Zanzibar takes 20 minutes. Alternatively, you can catch a ferry. From Stone Town, it's an hour by road to Matemwe Retreat.

Who to contact
Visit your local travel specialist, e-mail *matemwe@asilialodges.com* or go to *www.asilialodges.com*

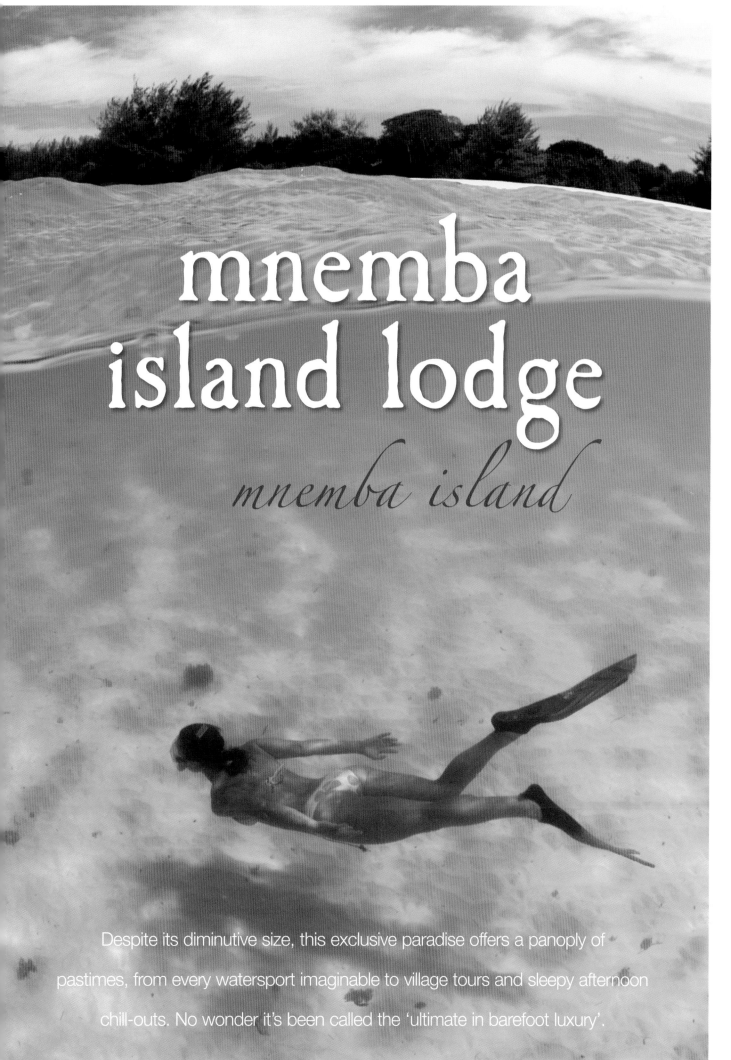

mnemba
island lodge

mnemba island

Despite its diminutive size, this exclusive paradise offers a panoply of pastimes, from every watersport imaginable to village tours and sleepy afternoon chill-outs. No wonder it's been called the 'ultimate in barefoot luxury'.

As I removed my sandals and stepped off the boat onto talcum powder-like white sand, I felt gripped by the island's magic

PREVIOUS SPREAD The guest areas are open-sided and decorated with an eye to comfort.

Swimming in paradise.

THIS SPREAD The bandas, with their wide verandas and thatched roofs, beckon invitingly from beneath the tropical beach forest.

An informal evening on the beach.

Exploring the coastline on a dhow.

Dinner can be served on the beach.

Crisp linens, locally wrought furniture and outsized beds guarantee a restful stay.

Mnemba Island Lodge is situated on a small (just 1.5 kilometres in circumference), exclusive islet that lies four kilometres off the north-eastern tip of Zanzibar's main island. Boarding the lodge's small motorboat, I was transferred across a deep blue channel to one of the most romantic islands I have ever seen.

As I removed my sandals and stepped off the boat onto soft, talcum-powder-like white sand, I felt gripped by the island's magic. My feelings were echoed by a fellow passenger, a 12-year-old girl who, with her family, was also visiting Mnemba. 'I could live here forever,' she said.

Smiling staff members were there to welcome us, with a refreshingly chilled drink and an ice-cold, island-scented towel. I was shown to my divinely simple but luxurious banda, one of just 10 at Mnemba. Each is built using indigenous materials, such as traditional Zanzibarian palm matting. Inside, the beds have ornate headboards that are carved with the intricate, scrolled designs typical of the skilled craftsmanship prevalent throughout Zanzibar. Each banda is shaded beneath the tropical beach forest, and has a spacious veranda. Private bathrooms, with shower and basin, are reached via palm-lined walkways. Guest areas are all open-sided, and include a dining room, a sitting room and bar, and a small library.

Mnemba (its name means 'octopus head') is thought to be the remnant of a much larger island that was surrounded by a ring of reefs, forming a coral atoll. Today, a protection zone surrounds the island, conserving these magnificent and endangered reefs where giant turtles visit and spectacular tropical fish drift through the lagoons.

The lodge has a world-class dive centre run by the dedicated team of Jan and Leen Christiaens. Unable to resist their enthusiasm, I decided to dive the house reef with Leen. We boarded the boat and had no sooner got underway when we were joined by a pod of bottlenose dolphins. In a flash, we donned our masks and fins and slipped into the silvery ocean. The dolphins were in a playful mood, and three curious individuals in particular nosed us closely as they investigated the newcomers to their world. We swam with the elegant creatures for some minutes before they disappeared into the ultramarine depths.

On our return to the lodge, we were treated to a meal made from the freshest ingredients. A rainbow array of fish and lobsters is caught by local fishermen in traditional outriggers and delivered to the island daily, accompanied by baskets of fresh fruit and vegetables. All are put to good use by Smiley, the chef, whose speciality dishes are flavoured with a fusion of local spices. He'd prepared a barbecue on the beach, and, starving after our marine excursion, we tucked into a feast to remember. Above us, the African sky glittered with a million stars and, beneath our feet, the soft sand caressed our toes.

Later, replete and exhausted, we wandered off to our bandas to spend another perfect night in paradise.

details

When to go
Hot, humid conditions prevail, but are tempered by sea breezes. The best months to visit are from June to March.

How to get there
The lodge transfers guests from Zanzibar International Airport or Stone Town by road and boat.

Who to contact
Tel. (+27-11) 809 4300 or go to *www.mnemba-island.com* or *www.ccafrica.com*

pole pole resort

mafia island

A rarely visited conservation area on a balmy island off the coast of Tanzania

is the setting for one of the world's most exciting eco-lodges.

ANDREW WOODBURN

Raised on stilts, each luxurious unit has a Zanzibari bed for those essential afternoon siestas

PREVIOUS SPREAD Lamplit evenings on the beach at Pole Pole are popular with honeymooners.

THIS SPREAD The furniture is made of local wood and rattan.

Gentle giants – whale sharks are regular visitors to these waters.

The resort is situated in the Mafia Island Marine Park, famous for its coral reefs and mangroves. Each bungalow has its own veranda and en-suite bathroom.

The service is friendly, the food exquisite.

A romantic picnic beside the ocean.

A warm wind rustles the fronds of the coconut palm outside my veranda. Offshore, white-sailed dhows drift across the viridian waters of Chole Bay. It's a tranquil setting here at Pole Pole as the late afternoon light softens. I kick off my shoes and watch the moon rise and cast silvery fingers over the rippled ocean.

Pole Pole Resort (its name means 'slowly, slowly' in the Swahili language) has been hailed by the US *Travel & Leisure* magazine as one of the top 25 eco-lodges in the world. Its seven spacious en-suite bungalows are set in tropical gardens and were built by local craftsmen entirely of local timber. Raised on stilts, each unit has a private veranda with a Zanzibari bed for those essential afternoon siestas. Indoors, the bedlinen has been imported from Italy, the bathrooms have double basins and the showers are king-sized. Gauzy drapes hang at the windows. Beyond, there are endless views to the horizon.

The resort is situated inside Mafia Island Marine Park, one of the largest protected marine areas in the Indian Ocean. Founded in 1995, the reserve has gained international recognition as a centre of biodiversity for its coral reefs, abundant marine life, mangroves and coastal forests. The island is far off the tourist track, but for those who do make it here, it offers an experience they will never forget.

There's lots to do at Pole Pole. The underwater life is vibrant and plentiful – more than 400 species of fish have been identified – and the Mafia Island archipelago is a paradise for snorkellers and scuba divers. Whale sharks and manta rays also visit these waters. On land, the vegetation is just as lush. Large palm groves dominate, but there are also baobabs, mango and cashew trees, and mangroves that help to prevent coastal erosion. Wildlife includes vervet monkeys, small antelope, wild pigs, lemurs and many species of birds.

Apart from diving, Pole Pole offers dhow trips to various destinations around Chole Bay, with a favourite being the excursion to Fungo Marimbani, a strip of dazzling white sand that is revealed at low tide. Another popular outing is to Maweni, a coral reef easily accessed by snorkellers. And, when all those activities have left you with aching muscles, you can have an essential-oil massage in a palm-thatched banda or in a shady spot on the beach.

Dinners are a fusion of local and Italian dishes (attributable to the Italian owners). Tonight, lobster and king prawns are on offer. I opt for grilled barracuda and calamari, which are delicious. The food, my waiter tells me, is organically grown.

In the morning, I set off with a British honeymooning couple on a snorkelling trip. Our dhow first stops at Fungo Marimbani. 'We came here a few days ago for a picnic and had the whole place to ourselves. It was so romantic,' the wife tells me. 'We saw beautiful cowrie shells and so many crabs that we called it Crab City.'

After photographing a spotted jellyfish and two tiny white starfish, we continue to the reef where I waste no time jumping into the water. It's warm, and the clarity and colours are amazing. Hundreds of fish in all shades of the rainbow swim around the coral. I take a deep breath and kick down a few metres, floating free in the aqua paradise.

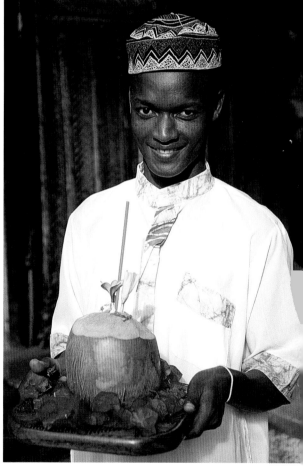

details

When to go
The resort is closed in April and May, when heavy rain falls. The most popular visiting period is from June to March.

How to get there
Daily flights connect Dar es Salaam and Kilindoni airstrip on Mafia Island. Resort staff will transport visitors to Pole Pole Resort.

Who to contact
E-mail *contact@polepole.com* or go to *www.polepole.com*

salome's garden
zanzibar island

This grand house was built by a sultan for his beloved daughter. Now fully restored as a hotel, its exotic décor, lavish detail and voluptuous gardens would please even modern-day royalty.

In my mind's eye, I can picture the sultan's daughter entertaining her suitors in these lush surroundings

The sun is setting, casting the swaying palm trees into stark silhouette as I arrive at Salome's Garden. It's a tranquil time of the day and Zanzibar's tropical heat has subsided with the cool evening breeze.

Situated on the beach at Bububu, on the island's west coast, Salome's Garden is a relaxed alternative to hotels in bustling Stone Town. 'My name is Tito,' says the manager, offering me a warm handshake. 'Our place runs like a private home. We have a cook, a waiter, driver, housekeeper, gardener and watchman. And they're all working for you.'

Salome's Garden was built in the mid-1880s by Sultan Said as a home for his beloved daughter. It was completely refurbished in 1997 and, with its lovely old furnishings and historical links adding a sense of stepping back in time, the house now operates as a guesthouse. There are just four airy bedrooms, sleeping a maximum of 10 people. All are decorated with exotic Zanzibari and colonial antiques, Persian carpets and lamps from India and Turkey. Upstairs, a guests' lounge displays artefacts from Sultan Said's era, including a crown that belonged to Princess Salome.

Outside, seven hectares of enclosed private gardens surround the villa. I set out to explore them, and walk past a small mosque into a tapestry of colourful plantings separated by ancient coral walls. Behind the house is a large orchard of fruit trees – mangoes, bananas, coconuts, papaya, oranges and tangerines. I stop to photograph an intricately carved wooden door and a Persian bath, now restored to a swimming pool. In my mind's eye, I can picture the sultan's daughter entertaining her suitors in these lush surroundings.

Salome's Garden is the ideal location from which to explore the rest of the island. There are several popular day tours that should not be missed. Swim with the dolphins from the southern village of Kizimkazi, or take one of the island's popular spice tours. Northern Zanzibar can easily be visited on a day excursion, as can the idyllic east coast beaches of Paje, Bwejuu and Jambiani.

I wake before sunrise and wander down to the beach. The fishermen emerge from their shelters to a gusty day and look out to sea disconsolately. 'Cannot go fishing,' says one of the men sadly. Another fisherman makes the most of the inclement weather by varnishing his boat.

I decide to visit Stone Town, and hop aboard a crowded *dala-dala*. I alight at the main market where fruit and vegetable vendors sit behind heaps of tomatoes, oranges, peppers, bananas and sweet potatoes. The air is heady with the fragrance of vanilla, cloves, cinnamon, cardamon, nutmeg and coriander. In the fish market, sleek kingfish and dorado are laid out next to mounds of small silver fish, octopus, squid and red snapper. I browse through the boutiques and craft shops, and pause to admire the famous wooden doors and unique blend of Arabic, Indian, African and European architecture. Entering the labyrinth of narrow winding alleyways, I am greeted by smiling children and loud shouts of *'jambo'*.

PREVIOUS SPREAD Seven hectares of tropical gardens surround Salome's Garden.

One can gaze for hours at the view across the swaying palms.

THIS SPREAD Meals are often served on the sunny veranda that runs the width of the house.

All manner of craft lie anchored off the beach at Bububu.

The hotel is furnished with Zanzibari antiques and Persian carpets.

Artwork for Africa at the Stone Town market.

The four bedrooms are stylish and elegant.

details

When to go
The rainy months are April and May; June to August bring good weather; December and January can be very humid.

How to get there
From the airport, it is 20 minutes by taxi to Stone Town. Take a taxi, or *dala-dala*, to Bububu Beach. Follow the sign to Imani Beach Lodge, which is directly opposite the walled garden of the property.

Who to contact
Tel. (+39 051) 23 4974, e-mail *info@houseofwonders.com* or go to *www.salomes-garden.com*

coconut coast
mozambique

MARTIN HARVEY

Modern-day Mozambique is a country of hope and commitment. Its interior is dramatic. The islands strung along its seaboard, from sandy Bazaruto Archipelago in the south to the northerly, far-flung emerald isles of the Quirimbas, are a haunting combination of historical memories, palm-fringed beaches and exceptional bird- and wildlife. The island lodges combine sensitive ecotourism with plush comfort.

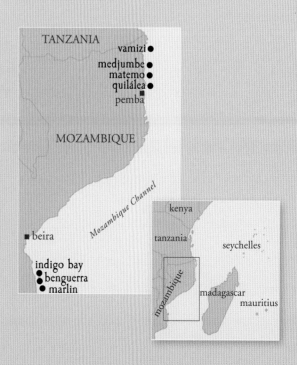

TANZANIA

vamizi ●
medjumbe ●
matemo ●
quilálea ●
pemba ●

MOZAMBIQUE

Mozambique Channel

■ beira

● indigo bay
● benguerra
● marlin

kenya

tanzania

seychelles

mozambique

madagascar

mauritius

Mozambique's islands are rich in birdlife.
There are numerous waders, including terns.

islands 47

benguerra lodge
benguerra island

The oldest lodge on a dramatic island,

Benguerra is a true paradise of ocean,

beach, forests and even dugongs.

In February 2007, Cyclone Favio swept directly over the pristine island of Benguerra off the coast of northern Mozambique, destroying everything in its path, from the beautiful 18-year-old Benguerra Lodge to the community projects it supports. Today, this admirable venture has risen from the devastation, and the resort owners have shown passionate determination to restore their beloved lodge and the life of the local villagers.

As I stepped off the motorboat onto the sandy shore, I was met with a big-smiled greeting. 'Welcome to Benguerra Lodge,' my host said. 'I've come to escort you to your villa.' We were led to an 'Exclusive Villa', and it certainly stood up to its name. A thatched roof covered golden and dark wood floors and furniture, an expansive bed sported fine white sheets and colourful cushions, and beautiful examples of local artwork caught my eye. The bathroom had twin basins, and a bath and shower. The luxury suites also have outdoor showers, intricately tiled in African designs. The veranda was completely private, with a plunge pool and twin recliners. Hurricane lanterns were placed on all the balustrades lest I lose my way at night. Nothing had been overlooked.

I unpacked and strolled down to the beach. The staff and islanders who work at the lodge or fish for a living greeted me with big smiles. The sand was warm beneath my toes, and I gazed across the sea to the horizon, and saw the sails of dhows tacking and dipping in the tropical breeze. Looking back at the lodge, I could see what made people come back to it time and again. Because it's set on the forested side of the island, Benguerra Lodge is extremely sheltered. At its back, the trees ring with the sounds of birds, including hornbills and the elusive olive pigeon and Narina trogon. Red squirrels, suni and duikers

also dwell in its depths. The lodge is popular with newly-weds, who enjoy the solitude and the romantic picnics on the beach.

Once you've tired of gazing at the view and all that lolling on the beach, there are activities aplenty to keep you occupied. The archipelago is world-renowned for fly-fishing, deep-sea fishing and for its coral reefs. I elected to take a boat ride to Two Mile Reef, where, after donning snorkels and goggles, I slipped beneath the surface of the ocean to witness coachmen, fusilier, surgeon and snapper, and the endearingly named oriental and barred sweetlips. There are more than 2 000 species of fish, as well as 120 types of coral, and whales, dolphins and crustaceans. Dugongs and four marine turtle species ply these waters as well.

Another, unusual sight is the freshwater lakes on the island, which are home to a population of crocodiles. The Bazaruto Archipelago was once joined to the African continent, and the crocs date back to that time. 'There were hippos here until the 1950s,' my host told me, 'although they've died out now.' In 2000, Benguerra and its sister islands of Bazaruto, Magaruque,

PREVIOUS SPREAD The suites are welcoming and luxurious, with elegant furnishings and hurricane lanterns to illuminate the veranda.

You can round off a sunset cruise in a dhow with a romantic dinner on the beach.

THIS SPREAD Benguerra Lodge is popular with honeymooners.

Exploring the coastline.

The service is smiling; the drinks are heavenly.

Pansy Island has a proliferation of pansy shells. They may not be removed.

Looking back at the lodge, I could see what made people come back to it time and again

Banque and Santa Carolina were declared a national park, with its highlights including forest, savanna, wetlands and coral reefs. The islands are known for the ridge of high sand dunes that dominates the chain, and for their extensive tidal flats and inland lakes. There's an encouraging wealth of birdlife, including some 26 species of waders.

Dinner that night was served beneath the light of the stars and dozens of hurricane lanterns. My crab curry was superb, as were the cocktails made at the bar (a converted dhow) that preceded it and the fruits that followed. I returned to my villa and sank between those fine sheets, and remembered nothing until dawn touched my face the next morning.

After breakfasting on fresh fruit, I stroll to the beach and take a boat ride to Pansy Island. Here, on a sandy outcrop, are found hundreds of delicate pansy shells. No one is allowed to remove these shells, so I bend down carefully and click away to add them to my memory bank of this elegant wonderland.

Benguerra's owners are passionate about conservation and are dedicated to the involvement of the local community in sharing and conserving their island. Park levies included in guests' fees are used to support local resident communities with the establishment of schools and payment for teachers, sponsoring the education of a number of orphaned children and supplying food to the needy. The lodge has also enabled the community to develop gardens from which they supply food to both the villagers and the lodge. The initiative is called *Khani Kwedho* ('our home', in the local dialect).

And this particular home is a paradise.

The open-air shower, with its eye-catching pattern of mosaics.

Exploring the magical underwater world.

The sea air is a great appetite-stimulator.

Your own private piece of paradise!

Dinner that night was served beneath the light of the stars and dozens of hurricane lamps

BENGUERRA LODGE

BENGUERRA LODGE

details

When to go
The resort is open all year. The weather is good year-round, although it is rainy between December and April.

How to get there
Benguerra Island is just a few minutes by air from the mainland town of Vilanculos. A boat ride from the mainland will take about 30 minutes.

Who to contact
Tel. (+27-11) 452 0641, e-mail *benguerra @icon.co.za* or go to *www.benguerra.co.za*

marlin lodge

benguerra island

Mozambique's Bazaruto Archipelago is known as the 'crown jewels' of the western Indian Ocean, and Benguerra Island is considered by its inhabitants to be the diamond-encrusted tiara in the group. On its shoreline is a beautiful retreat – Marlin Lodge.

The speedboat streaked across the aquamarine waters of the Indian Ocean, passing graceful dhows and flocks of seabirds. Ahead lay Benguerra Island, an 11-kilometre-long, 5,5-kilometre-wide landmass that is the second largest in the Bazaruto Archipelago. On its western side, facing the African continent, lies the romantic Marlin Lodge.

Within minutes of arriving, I was led to my home for the next day or two, one of 17 west-facing chalets and suites that meander along the beach at Flamingo Bay. Mine was elegant, with air-conditioning and décor that was an appealing fusion of rustic style and soft, gauzy drapes. Crisp linen covered the bed, and a huge swathe of mosquito net ensured a good night's sleep ahead. I looked forward to spending some down time on the inviting deck-chairs that faced the sea on my own private balcony. More luxurious accommodation is also available, with the most sumptuous being thee executive suites, each with two lounges, twin vanity basins and both indoor and outdoor showers. All the chalets and suites have direct access to the beach.

After wandering along the shoreline, I took notice of the activities on offer. The archipelago offers some of the most challenging game fishing in the subcontinent, with striped marlin, sailfish, king and queen mackerel, giant barracuda and kingfish attracting keen anglers from around the world. Yachting day-trips are offered to deserted islands in the group; on arrival a romantic picnic is served – popular with newly-weds, I was told. There are also dunes to be scaled, a rich birdlife to be investigated and, of course, that quintessential Indian Ocean experience – a sundowner sail aboard a graceful dhow. I could see why Marlin Lodge is so appealing to honeymooners. The lodge also has a wellness centre, with internationally trained therapists. A variety of treatments are offered, including a massage on your own private balcony.

The following morning, I set off with a group of divers to Two Mile Reef. Donning snorkel and goggles, I slipped over the side of the boat and entered a coral fairyland with fishes in every hue known to man. Whale sharks and manta rays also visit this region, my guide told me, although none rewarded me with an appearance.

Some hours later, filled with tales of what we'd seen, we returned to the lodge. I was tired and hungry. After a shower, I strolled along the elevated wooden walkway to the dining area beneath a sky that was turning a velvety indigo, studded with uncountable stars. I dined beneath them on dishes whose flavours combined African, Asian and Portuguese elements. The chicken was sublime, the salads perfectly crisp.

Replete and yawning, I returned to my chalet and that irresistible big bed, and was soon dreaming of birds and fish and sails and wide smiles.

MARLIN LODGE (6)

PREVIOUS SPREAD Rich pickings await deep-sea anglers.

The harvest of the ocean is the focus of Marlin Lodge's menu.

THIS SPREAD The lodge's 17 chalets and suites line the beach at Flamingo Bay.

Diving at Two Mile Reef.

A balcony with a view.

An underwater world of delicate corals and multi-hued fish.

The rooms are spacious, stylish and comfortable.

The archipelago offers some of the most challenging game fishing in the subcontinent

DAVID ROGERS

details

When to go
The lodge is open all year.

How to get there
There's an international airport at Vilanculos, on the mainland. Benguerra lies 14 kilometres offshore and is accessible by boat.

Who to contact
Tel. (+27-12) 460 9410, e-mail *reservations@marlinlodge.co.za* or go to *www.marlinlodge.co.za*

quilálea
private island

quirimbas archipelago

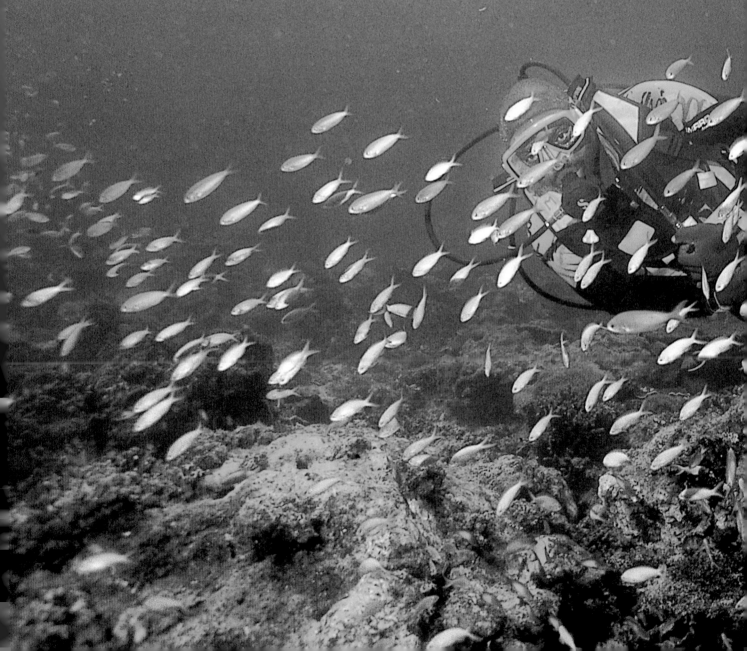

The Quirimbas Archipelago is the quintessential tropical
holiday destination, and the serene, completely private
island of Quilálea is one of the fairest of them all.

PREVIOUS SPREAD More than 350 species of fish have been identified in the waters around the Quirimbas Archipelago.

THIS SPREAD Exploring the mangrove-lined channels of Sencar Island.

Quilálea's villas are constructed of local materials and have been designed to maintain ecological integrity.

Dinner is served against a thatch-framed ocean view.

Hammocks suspended at the water's edge encourage quiet reflection.

The comfortable sitting room encourages guests to relax at the end of the day.

The word *lala*, which is the Swahili word for sleep, is derived from 'Quilálea'. Portuguese and Arab trading vessels once escaped the fury of the Indian Ocean storms by mooring in this sheltered landward side of the Quirimbas Archipelago. The trading ships no longer come, but today Quilálea Island invites visitors to relax in a private island sanctuary – the first of its kind – created in 2002 by John and Marjolaine Hewlett.

The 34-hectare island, one of some 30 in the far-flung Quirimbas, is fringed by sandy beaches, where ghost crabs scuttle and outcrops of coral have been beaten into fascinating shapes by the ocean. One of the inlets, Turtle Beach, is a regular breeding ground for green and hawksbill turtles. The island's interior is equally entrancing, with forests of baobabs, African star-chestnuts and corkwoods. Here are Suni antelope and bushbuck, along with scarlet sunbirds, Böhm's little bee-eaters, tchagras and many other birds.

The Hewletts have taken care to maintain the paradise in which they have built their retreat and the natural materials used in its construction came from the mainland. There are nine handcrafted villas with coral walls, palm-frond thatch, teak decks and mahogany doors. The rooms have been designed to catch the breeze and the scent of the sea.

The island has no freshwater source, so all water is purified in a desalination plant. It tastes perfectly good, and the lack of standing water means that there are no mosquitoes – Quilálea is one of the few islands in the archipelago that is malaria-free.

All my meals were excellently prepared by the chef, whose dishes fuse Mozambican, Portuguese and Goan cuisine.

Life at Quilálea is laid-back. On some afternoons, I sat at the upturned dhow that doubled as a bar, ordered a beer and a bowl of peri-peri cashew nuts and switched my gaze from my book to the pied kingfisher dive-bombing the

*The island is fringed
by sandy beaches, where
ghost crabs scuttle*

pool, then to the dhows out at sea. There is also satellite television and wi-fi connectivity, but it hardly seemed necessary.

The facilities include a registered diving school with scuba gear and instructors, a deep-sea fishing boat bristling with rods, speedboats and kayaks. On the main beach is a deep channel where dolphins are often seen, and on the nearby reef, Cabecas, we spotted nudibranches, moray eels and dozens of bluespotted ribbontails. There are many other pristine dive sites in and around the island. Fascinated by the marine life, I took a low-tide paddle through the latticework of channels at neighbouring Sencar Island, where five different mangrove species and innumerable seabirds are found.

Passionate about the underwater world, the Hewletts, along with a marine biologist friend, established a marine sanctuary, which was recognised by the World Wildlife Fund for Nature in 2001. One year later, the Quirimbas National Park was declared. The park incorporates Quilálea and Sencar islands in the marine sanctuary, as well as a zone of 'Total Protection', where fishing and marine harvesting are forbidden. The region is home to more than 350 identified species of fish, including parrotfish, angelfish and various moray eels.

Quilálea has been voted by the UK *Tatler* as one of its top 101 destinations worldwide, while the London *Sunday Times* reported that the island and its resort 'stand as a symbol of how tourism should be in an ideal world'.

It's hard to decide whether to focus on the never-ending view or the delectable cuisine before you.

The island's forested interior is home to numerous antelope species.

Quilálea from the air.

The bedrooms are large and comfortable. Although the beds are draped with netting, there are no malaria mosquitoes on the island.

On the main beach is a deep channel where dolphins are often seen

details

When to go
Quilálea is open all year.

How to get there
The island can be reached by helicopter from mainland Pemba, which has an international airport. Charter flights and boat transfers can be arranged.

Who to contact
Contact Classic Retreats, tel. (+27-11) 268 6236, e-mail *quirimbas@plexusmoz.com* or go to *www.quilalea.com*

rani resorts

matemo, medjumbe and indigo bay

Rani Resorts has perfected the art of pampering guests in exotic and unspoiled locations. Their footprint in southern Africa embraces some of the region's most amazing destinations, including the Victoria Falls and Mozambique. We feature the three Indian Ocean islands in their collection: Matemo Island and Medjumbe Private Island in the Quirimbas Archipelago off northern Mozambique, and Indigo Bay Island Resort and Spa on Bazaruto Island.

matemo island
quirimbas archipelago

Balmy days, a tranquil lodge, heavenly food and an underwater wonderland are

par for the course at Matemo, a coral paradise in a turquoise sea.

Matemo is one of the larger islands in the Quirimbas Archipelago, a chain of fossil coral rock islands that lies off northern Mozambique's beautiful coast. On landing, we were collected from the airstrip in a brightly painted *dagadaga* for the short drive to the lodge, and it immediately became evident that lots of fun would be had. As we arrived, I crossed the pool deck and looked over a wide and graceful bay; dhows, yachts and other small craft bobbed about on the clear blue water. Lining the beach, their doors opening onto the sand, was a string of 24 thatched chalets just metres from the warm Indian Ocean.

Even on this remote and tranquil island, the chalets offered all the comforts of a luxury hotel, with satellite television, air-conditioning, mosquito nets, mini bars and bathrooms with baths, as well as indoor and outdoor showers. The floors are wooden and the walls are hung with North African art.

After settling in, as the sun dipped over the horizon, I followed the other guests walking down the white beach towards the restaurant, where lanterns and candles lent a festive atmosphere. There was a terrific spread that included the day's catch of fish, prawns, calamari and lobster, as well as vegetable spring rolls, cream of pumpkin soup, crab curry, pasta, lamb chops, stir-fries, and a buffet of desserts and fresh fruit.

That night I mulled over the activities on offer; there were dhows for sunset cruises, motorboats for fishing, an activity centre offering waterskis, snorkelling gear, windsurfers and kayaks, and a certificated dive school with a range of options, from shallow six-metre dives off nearby Rolas Island to wall dives at Napoleon Wrasse Reef. Volleyball on the beach is another favourite pastime.

Matemo also has a village with tiny shops that offer a sense of daily life in Mozambique. The island is within view of Ibo – the historical isle that was once an important trading post for Portuguese seafarers. Guided trips are offered daily to Ibo and its fort, which dates back to the mid-1700s, and to its town, which includes the remains of what was once a fashionable, prosperous port with interesting examples of 19th- and early 20th-century Portuguese architecture.

PREVIOUS SPREAD A dhow glides gracefully across the turquoise sea.

THIS SPREAD A fishing charter boat lies at anchor off palm-lined Matemo Island. Apart from deep-sea angling, activities on offer include scuba diving, snorkelling, waterskiing, exploring in a kayak and land-based sports such as volleyball.

King-sized beds, muslin drapes and island-style furnishings.

The rustic exterior of the palm-thatched villas belies their luxuriously appointed interiors.

Matemo is a 20-minute flight from Pemba.

A bar beside the freshwater pool is a great place to unwind and compare the experiences of the day.

details

When to go
The resort is open all year.

How to get there
Matemo is a 20-minute flight from Pemba, which has an international airport.

Who to contact
Tel. (+27-11) 467 1277 or (+258-21) 71 5000, e-mail *reservations@raniresorts.com*, or go to *www.raniresorts.com*

The diving off Medjumbe is spectacular, with coral reefs and a multitude of fish in every colour just waiting to be discovered.

Meals are served beside the pool, overlooking the ocean. The food at the resort is highly rated.

Snorkelling in the calm, crystal-clear, aquamarine waters.

There are just 13 beach chalets, ensuring complete privacy and tranquillity.

The rooms are cosy and comfortable, with wooden floors, plush carpets and muslin-swathed, king-sized beds.

RANI RESORTS

medjumbe private island *quirimbas archipelago*

The living is easy at Medjumbe. The peace is tangible and the views are breathtaking.

Medjumbe Private Island is just 20 minutes by air from Matemo, and is just the island paradise you might imagine. It is a sliver of sand just a few hundred metres wide and roughly one kilometre in length, but at low tide, the water recedes to reveal a narrow sandbar that juts out like a thin white needle into the blue ocean.

Apart from the gracious, hospitable staff and maximum of just 26 guests (there are only 13 beach chalets), there are no other inhabitants on Medjumbe. Each chalet is cool with a delightful beach-house atmosphere, and has a palm-thatched roof, lime-washed wood, reed ceilings, blue and white soft furnishings and interesting collections of shells and other offerings from the sea. There's also satellite television, air-conditioning and mini bars, en-suite bathrooms and indoor and al fresco showers.

Lured by the glorious views, I wandered onto my private deck with its own plunge pool. Flocks of terns rose and fell like bright clouds against the blue sea. Herons stood statue-like, staring into the rock pools for signs of life. The temperature in the lagoon was 30 °C, and I wallowed happily, enjoying the bliss of doing nothing except watch the water, which was in a dozen shades, from pale blue-white in the shallows to shadowy ultramarine in the deep.

I decided to take advantage of the excellent diving. The Quirimbas offer spectacular marine life, and even at three metres I found myself surrounded by colourful corals and hundreds of small fishes. I investigated the Edge of Reason dive site, where at 30 metres (below me, the drop continued several hundred metres to the ocean floor) I marvelled at large gorgonian fans waving in the currents, schools of queen fishes and an inquisitive grouper of about 80 kilograms which approached to investigate our presence.

Night was falling as we returned to the lodge. The lamps were lit and a team of chefs was preparing an array of prawns, beef and fish fillets for a meal beneath the stars. It was just as paradise should be.

RANI RESORTS

details

When to go
The lodge is open all year.

How to get there
Medjumbe Private Island is about 40 minutes by air from Pemba, which has an international airport. It is a 20-minute flight from Matemo Island.

Who to contact
Tel. (+27-11) 467-1277, e-mail r*eservations@raniresorts.com* or go to *www.raniresorts.com*

indigo bay island resort and spa
bazaruto island

This is island life at its best: the weather is great, the pace is slow and the mood is utterly relaxing.

The light aircraft skims over the aquamarine waters, with dolphins breaking the surface and seabirds swirling above them. Below me lies the island of Bazaruto, its sand dunes rising to meet a light dusting of clouds. We land and I am greeted with a warm smile and a cool drink. I could get used to tropical getaways, I think, as I take in the never-ending views and simply stylish island resort of Indigo Bay.

I am shown to my beach chalet by Ndlua, a local islander with a fabulous smile. Quietly luxurious and just footsteps from the Indian Ocean, it has an en-suite bathroom with a generous bath from which there are uninterrupted views of the sea. A king-sized bed holds the promise of a good night's sleep. There is also a lounge, indoor and al fresco showers, air-conditioning, mosquito screens and satellite television. Higher up the shore, the Presidential and Bay View Villas have two bedrooms, two bathrooms, a spa bath, private swimming pools and expansive decks overlooking the bay.

Bazaruto Island is a 30-kilometre stretch of land that is the largest in the archipelago for which it is named. Together with the second- and third-largest islands, Benguerra and Magaruque, it once formed part of a peninsula that parted company from the African continent some 10 000 years ago. Now, the island is a tranquil destination for discerning guests, with lodges springing up along its shores.

After unpacking, I kick off my shoes, slip into a cool pareo and head to the beach. Scuffing the warm sand, I stroll along the water's edge, admiring the sails of dhows as they dip gracefully offshore. I investigate the activities on offer. There's diving and snorkelling, game fishing, sailing, water-skiing, windsurfing and kayaking. For landlubbers, there's tennis, golf, sandboarding, horseriding, island drives and a host of beach games.

I pick up my snorkel and goggles, and join a diving expedition headed for the nearby Turtle Reef. I slip over the side of the boat into a multicoloured world. I've seen many coral dive sites, but the sheer variety and vividness of the colours here entrance me. There are butterflyfish, painted surgeons, angelfish and numerous wrasse.

Back on the boat, the dive instructor tells me that it's a pity I'm not visiting a month later. 'At the end of July and in August, humpback whales arrive here from the Antarctic to bear their calves,' he says. Giant whale sharks and manta rays are also regular visitors, and the shallow waters are home to the extremely rare, grass-eating dugong.

I vow to return to Indigo Bay ... soon.

It's a short stroll from your beach chalet to the sea.

You can greet the day with a horseback ride along the water's edge.

There's a view of the ocean from every window. The chalets are carefully furnished for maximum comfort.

Dinner is served on the beach.

LIBBY EDWARDS (2)

RANI RESORTS

RANI RESORTS

details

When to go
The lodge is open all year.

How to get there
Vilanculos has an international airport, with daily flights from Johannesburg. Visitors are met by Indigo Lodge representatives and escorted to an air shuttle. If travelling to Vilanculos by road, private parking and a transfer to the airport are available.

Who to contact
Tel. (+27-11) 467-1277, e-mail *reservations@raniresorts.com* or go to *www.raniresorts.com*

vamizi

island lodge

vamizi island

A coral-ringed island, its beaches regularly visited by turtles, is the site of a first-class, eco-friendly lodge that offers all the creature comforts in serene surroundings.

At the northerly point of Mozambique's 3 000-kilometre-long coastline lies the Quirimbas Archipelago, a string of islands that rise from the Indian Ocean like a necklace of gems. Among these is Vamizi Island. Just 12 kilometres long and less than two kilometres wide, this pristine island was the preserve of local fishermen and a handful of scientists until 2006, when the Maluane Conservation Project, headed by businessman Christopher Cox and wildlife veterinarian Dr Julie Garnier, opened what is arguably the most luxurious lodge in the country.

I landed at the airstrip on the south-western side of the island, then was driven southwards through lushly forested countryside that is home to 132 bird species, including the western reef heron and the Madagascar bee-eater.

Six beaches on the island are regularly visited by turtles, which crawl up the sands to lay their eggs. The longest of these is in the north-west, where some eight kilometres of white sand shelve gently to provide the perfect venue for swimming and long walks. Tucked between the trees that form a sheltered backdrop is Vamizi Island Lodge, with 12 beach chalets each situated more than 70 metres apart.

Inside, the proportions are equally generous and I paced 25 steps from the bathroom, past the four-poster bed, into a lounge and onto the deck with its Indian Ocean views. A single, dramatic slab of marble divided the shower and basins, and at its foot was a crusty coral bed that, on closer inspection, revealed itself to be the softest grey rubber mat imaginable. Shutters at the windows were as intricately carved as those in a Zanzibar palace, and long saffron drapes billowed inwards, bringing with them the cool scent of the sea.

I walked down the beach and watched ghost crabs scuttle across my path

After settling in, I walked down the beach to the main dining area and watched ghost crabs scuttle across my path. Tables had been set up on the sand close to a fire. The food was outstanding. There were fresh salads flown in from South Africa, olives, a big platter of fish, including cod and red snapper, as well as buttered prawns, sashimi and a tray of sushi garnished with wasabi and ginger.

The resident scientist from the Cabo Delgado Biodiversity and Tourism Project, which is the scientific arm of the Maluane Project, gave a lecture in the bar that night. She discussed the work being done with the local community to control fishing practices, and told me that every morning scouts set off along the beaches to look for recently vacated turtle nests and to check for hatchlings that may have become entangled in mangrove roots. 'We found this one today,' she said, opening a basket to reveal a tiny turtle.

An Australian scientist who was conducting a coral census told me that the underwater gardens at Vamizi were as good as the best along his country's Great Barrier Reef and had been protected from the coral bleaching that has affected much of the Indian Ocean. I'd have liked to investigate for myself, but the weather dictated otherwise and, instead, I went fishing with a Frenchman and his two daughters. With a cigar clamped in his teeth and big seas all around us, he looked every bit like Ernest Hemingway.

PREVIOUS SPREAD The soft, warm glow of dozens of lanterns casts a romantic light over dinner tables set up on the sand.

THIS SPREAD Vamizi Island's tropical forest is home to 132 bird species.

The palm-thatched villas, built and crafted by local islanders, are furnished with king-sized beds draped in muslin and fitted with Egyptian cotton sheets.

Vamizi's eight kilometres of white, powdery beaches are popular with honeymooners.

Nothing compares to the thrill of landing a big game fish.

The main dining and sitting area.

details

When to go
The lodge is open throughout the year.

How to get there
There is an airport at Pemba, from which it's some 60 minutes by air to Vamizi Island.

Who to contact
For more information, tel. (+27-11) 884 8869, or contact *reservations@maluane.com*, or go to *www.maluane.com* or *www.vamizi.com*

malagasy magic

madagascar

Palm-fringed paradise.

Enigmatic Madagascar is a true treasure island. From its variegated turquoise waters to its emerald rice paddies and towering granite peaks, the Malagasy scenery is superb. Its wildlife is unique, with liquid-eyed lemurs and spiny tenrecs. Tiny islets hug the island. On these, a number of idyllic resorts offer excellent facilities, five-star food, smiling service, complete privacy and vast stretches of untouched beaches.

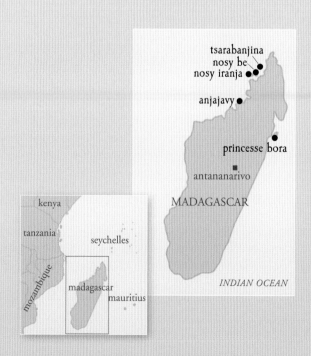

tsarabanjina
nosy be
nosy iranja

anjajavy

princesse bora

antananarivo

MADAGASCAR

kenya

tanzania

seychelles

mozambique

madagascar

mauritius

INDIAN OCEAN

anjajavy l'hôtel
north-west coast

Madagascar is a magical destination. At its

north-western corner is a lodge that exemplifies

the very essence of this tropical wonderland.

We explore underground caves the size of cathedrals, and take a night walk by torchlight in search of the diminutive mouse lemur

PREVIOUS SPREAD A Coquerel's sifaka in the gardens at Anjajavy L'Hôtel.

Forests tumble to the shoreline and the exquisitely warm water.

THIS SPREAD In Moromba Bay, a coral *tsingy* has been shaped into a mushroom by the sea.

The pool is surrounded by well-maintained gardens.

Dinner is served beneath the stars.

The villas have been decorated to guarantee the comfort of guests.

Anjajavy L'Hotel is surrounded by forest and beach.

'Teatime at the Oasis,' Hilton Hastings promised, 'is not to be missed.' So, obediently, I arrived in good time. While waiting, I busied myself with photographing the hotel's extraordinary landscaped gardens, with their striking water feature, exuberant climbing plants, lawns and a multitude of birds and reptiles. Like the hotel, the garden is a gloriously sophisticated celebration of the Eden that is Madagascar.

But the best was yet to come. As the staff brought in their trays of pre-dinner beverages, the primates arrived. First a troupe of common brown lemurs ran across the grass, followed by Coquerel's sifakas, with their delightfully ungainly loping motion.

Anjajavy L'Hôtel is a 25-chalet resort located in north-western Madagascar. Named for the nearby village (home to a host of mangrove *jajavy* trees), it is surrounded on three sides by deciduous and mangrove forests, and on its west by the Indian Ocean. It has considerable pedigree as a hotel. Owned by Frenchman Dominique Prat, and managed by Hilton Hastings, it has, despite its extremely remote setting, maintained the high standards of dining and service that are expected from establishments that fall under the banner of the exclusive Relais & Châteaux hotel group.

The double-storeyed, thatched suites are constructed of solid rosewood, with a double bed downstairs and two in the loft. All are fully air-conditioned and spacious, and offer fine views of the sea.

There are many ways to spend the day, from simply relaxing at the 200-square-metre swimming pool or strolling through the forest to kayaking, fishing, sailing or a massage. Thousands of hectares of state-owned forests surround the resort. Of these, some 450 hectares are managed and protected by the hotel, and the management is committed to planting hardwoods, building firebreaks and maintaining paths: a commitment that earned the hotel the 2005 Relais & Châteaux award for conservation.

I acquire the services of a guide, and explore the thick forests and coastal mangroves. We explore underground caves the size of cathedrals, and take a night walk by torchlight in search of the diminutive mouse lemur. 'There are more than 1 800 floral species here,' said my Malagasy guide. The birdlife is rich, too, with the names of just about every species of swift, kingfisher, quail, bee-eater and coucal we see starting with the word 'Madagascar'.

Early one morning, armed with a picnic, we set off in the 10-metre motorboat for Moromba Bay, a world of small coves and jagged limestone outcrops, or *tsingy*. Some are deeply eroded at their base and rise from the sea like mushrooms. They provide an excellent foothold for plants and three types of baobabs. As a bonus, I spot Madagascar fish-eagles.

I return to dinner on the beach. The tables are exquisitely decorated with flowers and lanterns, and I tuck into grilled lobster, mangrove crab and the best chocolate ice cream in Madagascar.

Anjajavy is one of the most striking places I have ever visited, and it's good to know that the lodge, its visitors and the French NGO *Ecoles du Monde* association support educational facilities for some 160 children in the Anjajavy and neighbouring Ambondro Ampassy communities.

details

When to go
The lodge is open all year.

How to get there.
The lodge is a 90-minute flight from Antananarivo.

Who to contact
E-mail *contact@anjajavy.com* or go to *www.anjajavy.com*

constance lodge tsarabanjina

nosy mitsio archipelago

The only sounds you'll hear at this Malagasy paradise are the call of the

seabirds and the gentle swish of the ocean. Pack nothing but your passport,

your beachwear and a desire for a complete break from civilisation.

I had been on the ocean for an hour after leaving the busy port of Hell-Ville, Nosy Be. We were travelling in a north-westerly direction with the Madagascan mainland sketched against the eastern horizon. The sea, its deep azure blue upset by large, choppy swells, reminded me of something an old French sailor had told me: 'Look out for the area north-west of the mainland, monsieur. It is often affected by the trade winds.'

Standing up to stretch my limbs and inhale the fresh ocean breeze, I was rewarded with the sight of the Nosy Mitsio archipelago, easily distinguished by Les Quatre Frères (four islets of silver basalt) and the other larger, neighbouring islands, Nosy Tsarabanjina being the closest. As we entered the shallows around the island group, the water began to change colour, turning a clear, shimmering turquoise. Suddenly a spinner dolphin leapt out from the bow wave of our boat, followed by a second. As quickly as they had appeared, the pair turned and sped off into the depths. What a wild welcome to Tsarabanjina!

Landing on the island's southern white beach, I stepped onto the grainy white coral sands. A staff member greeted me with a wide smile, a long, cool drink and an ice-cold towel, and showed me to the A-frame chalet that would be my home for the next few days. Made from local materials, each element of the building was designed to gain the maximum shade and protection from the elements. Just a stone's throw in front of the chalet was the sea, where coral-reef fish, turtles and rays roamed the shallow, transparent waters.

The name Tsarabanjina apparently means 'good to look at' in the local language. If true, it's a major understatement. This island is more than simply good to look at. In fact, with its volcanic rock formations in black, red and grey rising high in its centre and the voluptuous green vegetation that includes baobabs, pachypodiums and a myriad other plants, Tsarabanjina is a treat for the eyes. Below the belt of green are natural coral outcrops and arches, and three white beaches that open to the crystal-clear, indigo-blue and green waters of the warm Indian ocean.

At Tsarabanjina, even finding your meals or the bar is an adventure. I left my room and strolled along the beach, following a well-worn path over natural volcanic rocks beneath eroded coral cliffs to a small, private beach. There I found, completely hidden from prying eyes, the double-storeyed dining and bar area. The views are superb. Guests are instructed to leave their shoes and sandals at the base of the steps before entering the area, the floor of which is covered in white powdery sand. It's the perfect place to sip dark and stormy drinks of rum and ginger beer or exotic cocktails.

Here, while listening to Raoul strumming his guitar, guests can recollect the underwater wonderland they've explored during the day, or simply chill out and soak up the laid-back atmosphere.

PREVIOUS SPREAD Tsarabanjina island is small and breathtakingly beautiful.

THIS SPREAD At each chalet, a shaded hammock is suspended seductively above the hot white sand, while recliners at the water's edge encourage guests to perfect their tans.

A path of volcanic rock leads to an atmospheric bar.

Well-appointed bedrooms ensure a good night's sleep.

Tsarabanjina offers a wide range of watersports.

The A-frame chalets have en-suite bathrooms.

A staff member greeted me with a wide smile, a long, cool drink and an ice-cold towel

details

When to go
The resort is open all year.

How to get there
Tsarabanjina lies 40 nautical miles from Nosy Be, and is accessible by seaplane or speedboat (a 90-minute ride).

Who to contact
Tsarabanjina is a member of the Constance Hotels Experience, tel. (+261-320) 51 5229, e-mail *lodges@constancehotels.com* or go to *www.tsarabanjina.com*

nose be hotel

nosy be island

Situated on an island whose charms have been sung for some 350 years, Nosy Be Hotel has all the ingredients of the quintessential tropical holiday – great accommodation, a host of activities, excellent ocean views and food that will transport you.

The gardens turned out to be a source of real entertainment, with their huge variety of chameleons, lizards and geckos

Nosy Be, 'Big Island' in the Malagasy language, is the largest in the small archipelago that appears to have been tossed randomly into the sea off the north-western coast of Madagascar. Blessed with an almost perfect climate, its attractions were recognised as far back as 1649, when an English colonel, Robert Hunt, wrote: 'I do believe, by God's blessing, that not any part of the world is more advantageous for a plantation, being every way as well for pleasure as well as profit, in my estimation!'

I'd landed at Fascene International Airport, where I was collected and driven some 10 kilometres through verdant forests and past plantations and villages to the hustling, bustling Hell-Ville T-junction. Forgoing the left-hand turn to this busy town (named for one Admiral de Hell rather than a comment on conditions at the town itself), we turned right on to a winding road that meandered gently inland. Before I knew it, we'd arrived at the entrance to the secluded and sleepy Nosy Be Hotel.

Emerging from the car, I was struck immediately by the hotel's architecture – wooden elements are very much in evidence – and the pervasive aroma of vanilla that hovered in the air. The hotel is set in two hectares of luxuriant tropical gardens that are vibrant with blooms of frangipani, flamboyant and hibiscus. Nestled between the trees are five bungalows, each secluded and private, with 22 rooms. The bungalows have been decorated in different styles, but all integrate typical Malagasy culture and aesthetics. The emphasis at the hotel is on courtesy and comfort, and the rosewood, coconut, raffia and soft fabrics used to decorate the rooms are sensual and warm. The food is superb and the vanilla prawns and the black chocolate mousse, both house specialities, are sublime.

After unpacking. I set off for the beach. I'd gone just a few metres when I became aware of the uncomfortable sensation that I was being watched. Turning to investigate the source of my discomfort, I realised that I was being observed by a 30-centimetre-long chameleon of the most unlikely vivid turquoise-blue. It sat on a branch, eyeballing me in the rotating, slightly comic fashion of chameleons everywhere. On closer inspection, the gardens turned out to be a source of real entertainment, with their huge variety of chameleons, lizards and geckos just waiting to be found.

Nosy Be Hotel is the perfect base from which to explore all the island's special secrets. I booked a day trip to Nosy Komba and Nosy Tanikely, two islands to the south-east. Komba means 'lemur' in the Malagasy language, and I was thrilled to see the threatened black lemurs in some of the island's last remaining indigenous forests. I visited the local fishing community and bought vanilla and unusual, attractive lace tablecloths, curtains and bedspreads.

Nosy Tanikely is a much smaller island, with marine reserve status, and I felt like a modern-day Robinson Crusoe in my own tropical retreat. Happily exploring, I stumbled upon secluded beaches and impressive cliffs with nesting tropicbirds. I pulled on my snorkel and goggles and took to the warm water. There, fascinated by the wonderland of corals, anemones, turtles and reef fish of every colour and size, I knew I was in paradise.

PREVIOUS SPREAD A shellfish spread proffered with Malagasy warmth.

The setting sun casts a sparkling path on the ocean.

THIS SPREAD Nosy Be's swimming pool is surrounded by tropical gardens.

Nosy Tanikely has marine reserve status, and is home to coral reefs and a prolific underwater life.

Nosy Be's bar lounge.

A female black lemur on Nosy Komba.

Rosewood and rattan furniture is combined with the finest fabrics.

details

When to go
Nosy Be Hotel is open all year. The cyclone season is in
February and March, and August and December bring increased
numbers of holidaymakers.

How to get there
There are regular flights from the mainland to Nosy Be's airport.
Contact your local travel agent.

Who to contact
Tel. (+261-20) 860 6151, e-mail *elma.ross@nosybehotel.com*
or go to *www.nosybehotel.com*

nosy iranja lodge
north-west coast

Nosy Iranja's owners are
passionate about preserving
the island's natural beauty,
proud of the local turtle-
monitoring project and dedicated to ensuring memorable
holidays for their visitors.

It's early morning in northern Madagascar as our speed-boat bumps over the swells. In the east, the horizon is turning a deep shade of orange. Dawn breaks as I step onto the tranquil shores of Nosy Iranja, and the sun casts a warm glow over the coconut palms. 'Welcome to Nosy Iranja Lodge,' says manager Claudia Rabenarivo, who is on the beach to meet me. 'It's a perfect moment to arrive.'

Nosy Iranja comprises two islands that are reached by boat from Nosy Be on the north-western coast of Madagascar. The lodge that bears the island's name is set in 13 hectares of tropical gardens on the southern island. This idyllic getaway, surrounded by translucent turquoise waters and soft white beaches, is the essence of barefoot luxury. Its 28 chalets are built of wood and other natural materials. Each has its own veranda and sea view, and is linked to the restaurant and reception area by sandy pathways.

Outdoor enthusiasts will find plenty to do. There's game fishing, sailing, waterskiing, snorkelling, scuba diving, windsurfing, kayaking, parasailing, pirogue trips and daily outings to see dolphins. There's also a library, satellite television, Internet facilities, a health spa and a boutique.

After breakfasting on pineapple juice, croissants and fresh fruit, I hike with a guide to the northern island, accessible via a kilometre-long sandbank that is revealed

A pirogue sails offshore under the blue cloudless sky as we walk through the shallows to the local village

at low tide. A pirogue sails offshore under the blue cloudless sky as we walk through the shallows to the local village. '*Mbola tsara*,' a group of women greet us cheerily, studiously scrubbing their cooking pots. Scaling a hill, we reach a lighthouse and climb the stairs. The view of the sapphire sea and the white sandbank is spectacular. We pass fields of cassava, papaya, sugar cane, bananas and pineapples, then beat our way through the bush to a remote beach.

Meals at Nosy Iranja Lodge naturally focus on seafood and are always delicious. After a dinner of kingfish kebabs in coconut sauce, I head back to my bungalow. I leave my door wide open and, within minutes, I'm lulled to sleep by the soothing sigh of the ocean.

Waking before dawn, I walk down to South Point. Nosy Iranja is home to an ongoing turtle-monitoring project. For many years I've longed to see turtles in their natural environment, so I'm thrilled to find a female green turtle returning to the water after laying her eggs. I'm just in time to click a few pictures before she splashes into the surf.

Pink ripples of cloud spread across the sky as daybreak approaches. In the soft light, I see Ignace, the turtle man, beckoning me. 'Come quick!' he says, 'a nest is hatching!' I hurry across to see 60 tiny turtles scrabbling along the sand. I photograph the spectacle, but the hatchlings have no time to pose for photogaphs. Their little flippers flap frantically as they scramble to get to the ocean. A wave washes over them and they're flung around in the foam. Escaping from the frothy surge, they swim free into the blue beyond. 'Bon voyage!' I wish them silently.

PREVIOUS SPREAD At Nosy Iranja, there's plenty to keep watersports enthusiasts occupied.

Turtle hatchlings scramble to reach the safety of the sea.

THIS SPREAD Nosy Iranja's northern island is accessible at low tide, when a sandy spit connecting the two islands is revealed.

The beaches are exquisitely peaceful.

The bungalows are furnished with an emphasis on stylish comfort.

A warm Malagasy smile and a fruity drink.

Dolphins are regular visitors to these waters.

details

When to go
Heavy rains and cyclones occur between January and March. It's best to visit between June and August, when humidity is lowest.

How to get there
There are direct flights into Nosy Be and the lodge owners will arrange to fetch you at the airport. From there, it's a 30-minute drive to the speedboat launch site, and a 75-minute ride to Nosy Iranja.

Who to contact
Tel. (+27-11) 806 6888, e-mail *hotels@legacyhotels.co.za* or *reservation.iranja@ blueline.mg*, or go to *www.legacyhotels.co.za*

princesse bora

ile sainte marie

Ile Sainte Marie and its waters brim with beauty, from tree-smothered plains to sparkling waterfalls and excellent beaches and, in July, the inimitable sight of humpback whales, which arrive to bear their young.

hotel

I pass crystalline water-falls, long white beaches and children somersaulting off coconut palms

PREVIOUS SPREAD A sunset flushes Ile Sainte Marie and its ocean with shades of red and orange.

THIS SPREAD Each villa has a wide veranda from which to view your private patch of paradise.

The shallows around Ile Sainte Marie are ideal for snorkelling.

Humpback whales visit these waters between July and September to calve.

Malagasy-style hospitality.

Treasures await at every turn, and a bicycle is the best way to see them.

Arriving at Ankarenar airport, on the southern tip of Ile Sainte Marie, I was met by a rocking zebu oxcart painted with whales and tropical fish. Never one to shy away from a new experience, I slung my luggage aboard and hopped on after it. We set off at a gentle pace, and rolled along a palm-lined road, its verges flanked by huts of local bamboo and palms.

Ile Sainte Marie is a beautiful, unspoilt island that lies in the lee of Madagascar's east coast. Protected by coral reefs from the sharks that patrol these waters, the long, narrow island is a haven of pristine beaches, and has seen little in the way of development. It once served as a refuge for pirates; today, there's little to threaten visitors.

Princesse Bora Lodge, on the island's south-west coast, is owned by the charismatic Francois-Xavier Mayer, whose ancestors, Charles, Napoleon and Nemours de Lastelle, arrived in Madagascar in 1825. Sailors on the way to the Indies, they fell in love with the island and decided to stay. Years later, one of their descendants created the lodge. 'Simplicity as real luxury,' is how Francois-Xavier describes his family's legacy. And the lodge certainly is a legacy to treasure. Built in the Sainte-Marienne tradition of local stone, wood and thatch, the lodge's villas lie at the edge of a lagoon. The beautiful main building is a series of wooden houses interconnected with walkways; the service is excellent, in big-smiled Malagasy style.

There's so much to see. After unpacking, I collect one of the lodge's motorcycles and go exploring. Nearby is the island's main town, Ambodifotatra. With little development and virtually no traffic, it is great fun and very safe. The past is everywhere – in the Catholic church built in the French style, and in the graveyard, where a skull-and-crossbone-engraved headstone recollects the island's infamous visitors. Heading further north, I pass crystalline waterfalls, long white beaches and children somersaulting off coconut palms. I end up at Coco Bay, which is owned exclusively by the Mayers, who describe it variously as 'the most beautiful place in the world', 'magic', 'the life of Robinson' and 'the dream'. Here you can relax in total privacy, with 2000 coconut palms and alongside your very own tropical aquarium.

I stop at the beach and perch on a huge basalt boulder. Sipping fresh coconut juice, I am startled by a large splash in the channel between the mainland and the bay. There, near the shore, is a group of humpback whales. Later, I'm told that the whales migrate from Antarctica and arrive in Malagasy waters between July and September. They come here to give birth and to mate, and remain in the protected channel for four months until their calves have grown big enough to return to the waters of the South Pole to stuff themselves with krill.

Back at Princesse Bora, guests can whale-watch from the lodge under the tutelage of Francois-Xavier, who is passionate about the creatures' conservation. He is the founder of Megaptera, an international association for whale protection, and visitors are encouraged to participate in scientific whale observation. It's a unique opportunity to learn and contribute to the research data pertaining to this great mammal.

details

When to go
The weather is mild between April and October. Summer (November to March) is hot and wet. July to September is the best period for whale-watching.

How to get there
Ile Sainte Marie can be reached from the Malagasy mainland by air (Air Madagascar or private charter flight) or sea. Contact your local travel agent.

Who to contact
Tel. (+261-20) 570 4003, e-mail *bora@wanadoo.mg* or go to *www.princesse-bora.com*

the mascarenes
mauritius

Mauritius, together with the smaller islands of Réunion and Rodrigues, comprise the Mascarene Isles, a haven for honeymooners and the world-weary. The main island, Mauritius, or Ile Maurice, is a mesmerising blend of volcanic peaks, lush plains, sparkling beaches and colourful underwater coral gardens. The island's lodges offer everything the holidaymaker needs, and lots more.

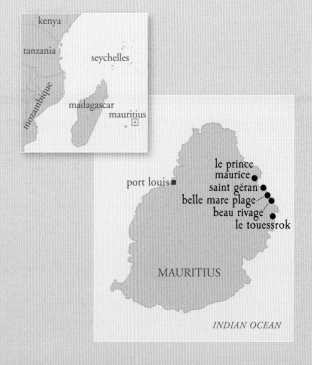

Storm clouds may bode bad weather, but the water's warm and there's still plenty to see beneath the surface.

beau rivage
east coast

This is the place to kick back, curl your toes in the sand and be spoiled with first-class cuisine. The resort is Beau Rivage, Naïade Resorts' flagship island retreat.

I may not be a food fundi, but I do recognise fine cuisine when I taste it. My meal of pan-fried scallops with *pleurote* (oyster mushroom) fricassée and caramelised fig carpaccio, followed by honey-glazed duck with preserved baby onions in five-spice liqueur, is a gastronomic sensation. Never have I eaten anything quite so delicious.

IndouChine is the signature restaurant at Beau Rivage, the flagship hotel of Naïade Resorts. Its fusion cuisine is created by executive chef Emmanuel Guémon, who is responsible for running the hotel's four restaurants. 'Here at IndouChine we have great fun creating unique tastes and adding a twist to our dishes while still respecting traditional French cooking techniques,' he says.

It is late afternoon when I arrive, and I'm welcomed with a vanilla-scented face towel, pineapple segments and an iced ginger drink. The soothing sounds of trickling water in an indoor pond introduce me to island time. I'm escorted to the Monsoon Bar, where communications co-ordinator Sandra Matooreah is waiting to meet me. 'Welcome to Beau Rivage,' she smiles, handing me a cocktail. 'We are not like other luxury hotels. Here you can really feel at home and our experience has been described as "barefoot five-star".'

Beau Rivage is located at Belle Mare, a spectacular stretch of sandy beach on Mauritius's east coast. With thatched-roof luxury suites spread around tranquil gardens, the hotel is well known for its tropical elegance and easy-going hospitality.

I'm welcomed with a vanilla-scented face towel, pineapple segments and an iced ginger drink

PREVIOUS SPREAD Good service, fine food and tropical splendour – Beau Rivage has it all.

The crystal-clear swimming pool lies between the hotel and the ocean.

THIS SPREAD The guestrooms are spacious and airy.

Lush tropical gardens surround the resort.

A pool, tiled in turquoise and sunshine yellow, welcomes visitors in the lobby.

Beach volleyball – popular with energetic guests.

Less strenuous beach activities include relaxing on recliners in the sun.

Apart from the fine food of IndouChine, Indian and Chinese cuisines are also on offer. In addition, there's the elegant Langoustier seafood restaurant, which offers a five-course 'seafarer' menu on Tuesdays. Club Savanne is a piano bar, popular with guests who have a liking for jazz and Cuban cigars.

Outdoor enthusiasts and sporty types will be in their element. There's windsurfing, waterskiing, scuba-diving, snorkelling, glass-bottomed-boat trips and deep-sea fishing. There's a gym and a spa, the largest swimming pool in the Indian Ocean, and facilities for beach volleyball, horseriding and tennis.

I take an excursion to Ile des Deux Cocos, a private island belonging to Naïade Resorts. Located in Blue Bay Marine Park, the island is a 45-minute trip by boat and the offshore coral reef boasts some of the best snorkelling in Mauritius. As we leave, bad weather blows in from the east. We speed across the choppy sea and salty spray soaks us within seconds. As we land, the clouds break and a blue sky beckons.

The only building on Ile des Deux Cocos is a white villa, built more than 100 years ago by Sir Henry Hesketh Bell, one of the first British governors to Mauritius. Sir Hesketh enjoyed the good life and the house was the scene of many hedonistic parties. Today, it's a popular venue for weddings.

After visiting the villa, I head off for a snorkelling trip. The marine life is plentiful and I watch parrotfish nibble on the coral, and beautiful butterflyfish, which always swim in pairs.

Back on shore, lunch is served – a delicious barbecue of chicken, lamb chops, tuna, marlin and prawn kebabs.

details

When to go
Mauritius is a year-round destination. The wettest months are from December to March, when occasional cyclones may occur.

How to get there
The hotel is situated 45 kilometres from the airport. The direct coastal road is not in good condition, so it is preferable to travel via the inland highway which takes about an hour. Take a taxi or arrange a chartered lift with White Sand Tours.

Who to contact
Tel. (+230) 402 2000, e-mail *brivage@naiade.com* or visit *www.naiaderesorts.com*.
White Sand Tours, tel. (+230) 212 3712 or e-mail *wst@whitesandtours.com*

constance
belle mare plage
east coast

Known for its warm atmosphere and challenging golf courses, Belle Mare Plage
has a clientele that returns year after year to enjoy its tropical charms.

It's a hot, sunny day and the relaxed holiday-makers are making the most of the weather. Topless tanners stretch out on beach recliners, offering their bronzed bodies to the sun. Hand in hand, a young couple ambles into the turquoise ocean. Beyond the jetty, waterskiers speed across the bay, kayakers paddle around a small island and a parasailer is outlined against the clear blue sky. Gentle waves lap the shore and I relax beneath a coconut palm, its fronds rustling softly above me.

Situated along a tranquil bay on the eastern coast of Mauritius, the Constance Belle Mare Plage is the ideal place for city folk to recharge their batteries. Glorious days in this picture-perfect setting encourage one to lie on the beach, or work on one's tan poolside, surrounded by lush, landscaped gardens.

Visitors who prefer sporty holidays won't be disappointed. The beautiful, two-kilometre-long beach is protected by an offshore coral reef that is ideal for snorkelling and a host of other watersports, including windsurfing, kayaking and waterskiing. Scuba-diving, catamaran excursions, parasailing and deep-sea fishing are available at an extra cost. There's also tennis, boules and beach volleyball.

However, golf is the sport for which Belle Mare Plage is best known. People staying here have free access to the hotel's two 18-hole championship courses, The Legend and The Links. 'People come to us specifically for the golf, but the added bonus is our friendly atmosphere,' says front office manager Jean-Francois Laurette. 'We have a high level of repeat guests; the Belle Mare Plage is like a second home for many of our visitors.'

Other facilities include a gymnasium, squash courts, Jacuzzis, a spa and a beauty centre.

The hotel has a wide range of accommodation. All rooms are stylish and modern, with a terrace or balcony. The deluxe suites have separate living rooms, and the ultra-luxurious presidential villa contains three bedrooms, a garden and private pool.

Guests have several options when it comes to meals. Among these, the main restaurant, La Citronnelle, serves themed buffets in the evenings. The beachside La Spiaggia serves Mediterranean cuisine during the day, and the Blue Penny Café is an exclusive à la carte, fine-dining restaurant.

I walk along the deserted beach as dawn begins to break over the milky ocean. Flecks of foam wash onto the shore and the sun breaks through the clouds, casting shafts of light across the water. It's been a while since I swung a club, but Belle Mare Plage seems like the right place to regain my golfing groove. I stroll over to The Legend course for a quick nine holes.

It's a scenic but testing layout with lots of ball-gobbling water features. Sadly, my game doesn't live up to expectations, so I chill out on the beach for the rest of the afternoon. Later, after a back massage at Le Spa de Constance, I'm rejuvenated and ready for a gourmet dinner at the Blue Penny Café.

My starter is wok-charred scallops with dill and crunchy vegetables, then I go for peppered pigeon breast served with pumpkin, fig and sweet-and-sour gravy. Dessert is a decadent chocolate ganache with rich praline and champagne mousse. Simply delicious.

PREVIOUS SPREAD Belle Mare Plage is known for its fine golf courses.

Deep-thatched guest areas surround the pool.

THIS SPREAD All guestrooms and suites feature private balconies with beautiful views.

Comfortable seating areas dot the hotel foyer.

The beach is a two-kilometre sweep of white sand.

Elegant, comfortable acommodation in a Junior Suite.

The Constance Belle Mare Plage combines rustic island charm with chic styling.

details

When to go
Mauritius is a year-round destination.
The wettest months are from December to March,
when occasional cyclones may occur.

How to get there
The hotel is situated on the east coast of the island.
Taxis or chartered rides can be arranged at the airport.

Who to contact
Tel. (+230) 402 2600, e-mail *resa@bellemareplagehotel.com* or go to *www.bellemareplagehotel.com* or
www.constancehotels.com

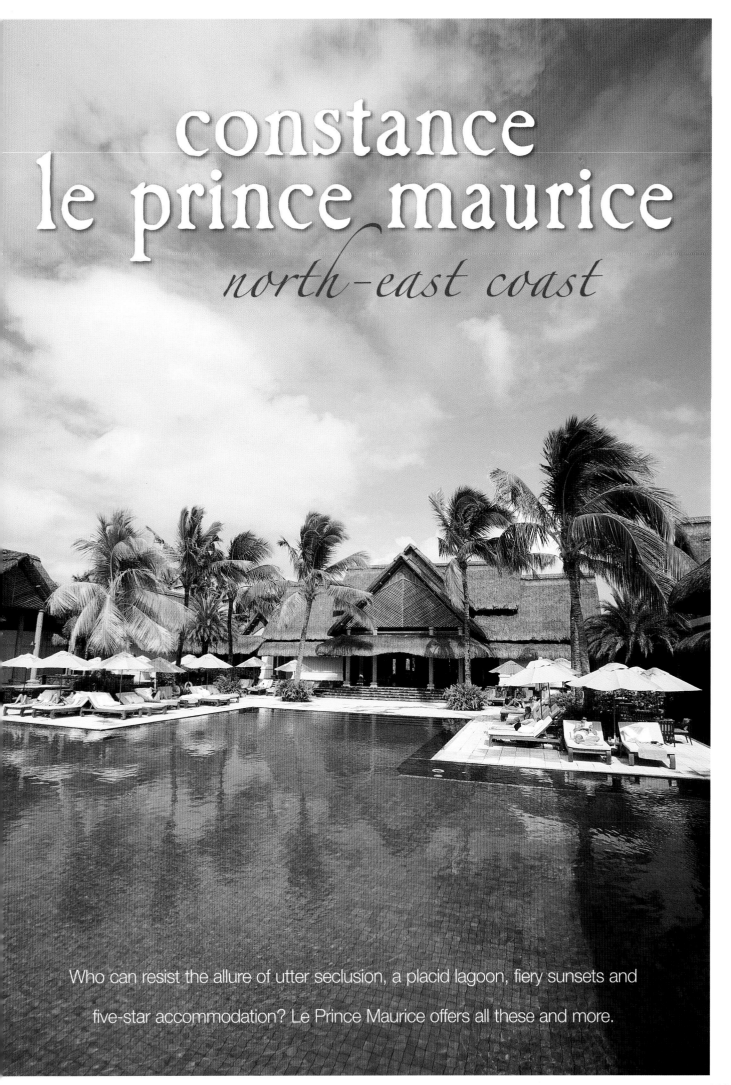

constance
le prince maurice
north-east coast

Who can resist the allure of utter seclusion, a placid lagoon, fiery sunsets and five-star accommodation? Le Prince Maurice offers all these and more.

Located on the edge of a tranquil lagoon, Le Barachois is the only floating restaurant on the island

PREVIOUS SPREAD Elegant accommodation and prime facilities attract guests time and again to Le Prince Maurice.

THIS SPREAD The floating restaurant of Le Barachois.

Some of the suites are built on stilts over a fish reserve.

A wide sweep of inviting tropical beach.

Condé Nast Traveller UK voted Le Prince Maurice as the 'Best Hotel for Food in the Indian Ocean'.

Walkways lead across sparkling pools to the communal areas.

A wooden walkway winds through mangrove trees to the most romantic restaurant in Mauritius. Located on the edge of a tranquil lagoon, Le Barachois is the only floating restaurant on the island. Enjoying a fine meal while suspended above the turquoise water is reason enough to make Constance Le Prince Maurice, a hotel of luxurious standards and relaxed atmosphere, your choice for a tropical holiday.

'What sets us apart from other hotels on Mauritius is our unique location,' says assistant manager Dalida Noëllis as we sit down for lunch at the restaurant overlooking the pool. 'Here you are far from the madding crowd; all you can hear is the sound of water. And, of course, we take great pride in belonging to the Relais & Châteaux collection of the world's finest restaurants and hotels.'

Situated on a secluded peninsula in 60 hectares of private land, and flanked by an azure lagoon, Le Prince Maurice has an idyllic location in north-eastern Mauritius. The white-sand beach is sheltered from prevailing winds and, at the resort's western side, there is a fish reserve.

The hotel has 89 thatched suites, some built on stilts over the reserve. Most regal of all is the Princely Suite, which has three bedrooms, an interior garden, three terraces and two swimming pools.

If you can tear yourself away from the languid life of leisure, there are watersports aplenty. Choose from windsurfing, snorkelling, kayaking, boat excursions or waterskiing. Other water activities, for an extra fee, are scuba-diving, deep-sea fishing and catamaran cruises. Land-based activities include tennis, cycling and squash. Golfers have free access to both The Legend and The Links golf courses at sister hotel, Constance Belle Mare Plage.

For the occasional rainy day, there is a library with plenty of reading material and DVDs. Or treat yourself to a massage, beauty or Ayurvedic treatment at the spa. Guests who enjoy cooking can attend the weekly culinary demonstration led by the executive chef, who will teach them how to prepare Mauritian dishes.

It is late afternoon when I walk across to the spa for a back massage. I'm led to an open-air treatment room where the masseur gets to work on my stiff muscles. Birds chirp and a soft wind rustles the palm fronds. The distant surf roars on the reef. Surrendering to my masseur's strong hands, I drift off to sleep.

Le Prince Maurice offers a range of local and international cuisine. Le Barachois, with its fine dining, five floating decks and uninterrupted views of the sinking sun, is undoubtedly the star of the restaurants, but L'Archipel, whose à la carte menu offers light, spicy dishes, and Le Beach Deck restaurant, on a wooden platform near the beach, are also excellent.

We walk along the romantic, lantern-lit walkway across the shimmering water to Le Barachois. The floating deck sways as our waiter brings me a starter of grilled scallops served with buckwheat seeds and a juicy orange salad. For the main course, I opt for grilled bream with crispy potatoes and steamed vegetables.

The next morning I reluctantly pack my bags. Unfortunately, it's time to leave this tropical paradise.

details

When to go
Mauritius is a year-round destination. The wettest months are from December to March, when occasional cyclones may occur.

How to get there
The hotel is situated on the north-eastern coast of the island. Taxis or chartered rides can be arranged at the airport.

Who to contact
Tel. (+230) 402 3636, e-mail *resa@princemaurice.com*. Go to *www.constancehotels.com* or *www.princemaurice.com*

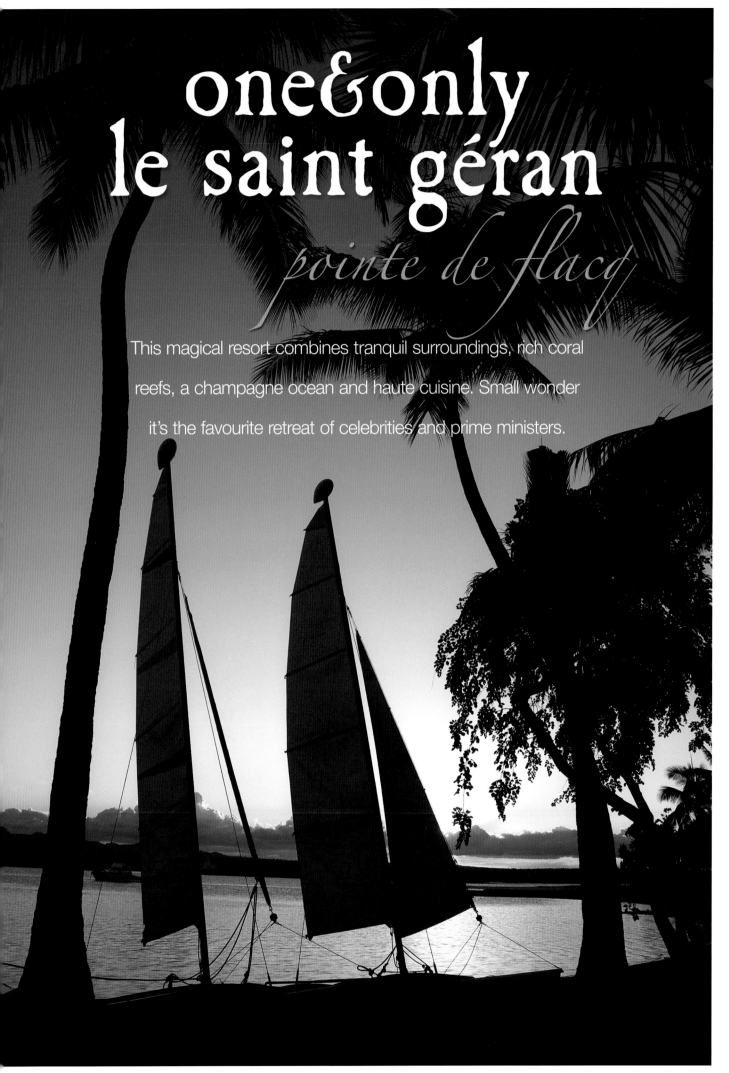

one&only
le saint géran

pointe de flacq

This magical resort combines tranquil surroundings, rich coral reefs, a champagne ocean and haute cuisine. Small wonder it's the favourite retreat of celebrities and prime ministers.

Just a few hours after landing in Mauritius, I'm a world away from the stresses and congestion of city life, ensconced in tropical luxury. After being escorted to my suite, I relax on the veranda and gaze at the coconut palms swaying gently in the warm breeze.

A few minutes later, there's a knock on my door. 'Welcome. I'm Ramjay, your butler. I hope you enjoy this complimentary cocktail; it's a mixture of citronella and watermelon juice. Can I unpack your bags for you? If there's anything you need, just press the "butler" button on the telephone.'

It's been a long day's travelling, so I exchange my jeans and track shoes for sarong and sandals and amble down to the beach. The air is balmy and the palms are silhouetted against the orange horizon. I plunge into the warm water for a sunset swim.

Situated on the east coast, Le Saint Géran, a member of the prestigious One&Only resorts group, lies on a private peninsula that encompasses a lagoon, beaches and tropical gardens. The hotel has been redesigned, and includes top-class restaurants, a spa and a Gary Player-designed golf course. Accommodation is in 163 rooms with terraces that face either the Indian Ocean or a tranquil lagoon. My suite has a king-sized bed covered with Egyptian cotton sheets and goose-down pillows. The softly lit bathroom tempts me into the tub with a range of soothing soaks enhanced with lavender, patchouli, eucalyptus and ylang-ylang oils.

Activities at One&Only Le Saint Géran are endless. You can scuba-dive, waterski, snorkel,

wind-surf, fish, or play golf or tennis. Once you've worked up an appetite, the world's finest food is on offer. Of the three restaurants, Spoon des Îles is best known as the creation of world-renowned chef Alain Ducasse. I dine at La Terrasse, where the service is prompt and unobtrusive, and nothing is too much trouble for the smiling staff. I tuck into chicken satay with grilled pickled pineapple, followed by swordfish with saffron rice. Down on the beach, honeymoon couples dine in romantic seclusion, their private chef grilling seafood on the coals.

I wake before sunrise and walk slowly down the deserted beach. Day breaks in a golden blaze and, after taking some photographs, I stroll back for breakfast. Later I head to the boathouse for a few hours of watersports. I haven't waterskied for 15 years, but it's like riding a bicycle, something you never forget. Then, after lunching on grilled fish at Paul & Virginie Restaurant, I board a glass-bottomed boat and motor out over clear aquamarine water. I don my mask and fins, and flop overboard to float suspended in the world of coral and marine creatures. The reef is alive with hundreds of tiny tropical fish, including checkerboard wrasse, butterflyfish and triggerfish. A soldier fish lies motionless on a coral ledge and aggressive brown damselfish stare at me and try to nip my legs.

As the sun sets, the vegetation glows in the golden light and the sea shimmers orange and red. It's an apt precursor for that evening's *sega* show, with its colourful, lusty dancing and lively music.

PREVIOUS SPREAD The suites are superb, with Egyptian cotton bedding and soft, goose-down pillows.

This is a quintessential tropical paradise retreat.

THIS SPREAD The choice of water-based leisure activities at the resort is intoxicating.

Recliners line the powdery beaches.

The perfect place to display your sporting prowess!

Lusty, vibrant *sega* dancers provide evening entertainment.

The furnishing and décor are stylish.

details

When to go
Mauritius is a year-round destination. The wettest months are from December to March, when occasional cyclones may occur.

How to get there
World Leisure Holidays exclusively represents One&Only Le Saint Géran and will arrange flights, transfers, accommodation and excursions.

Who to contact
Tel. (0860) 95 4954 or go to *www.wlh.co.za*

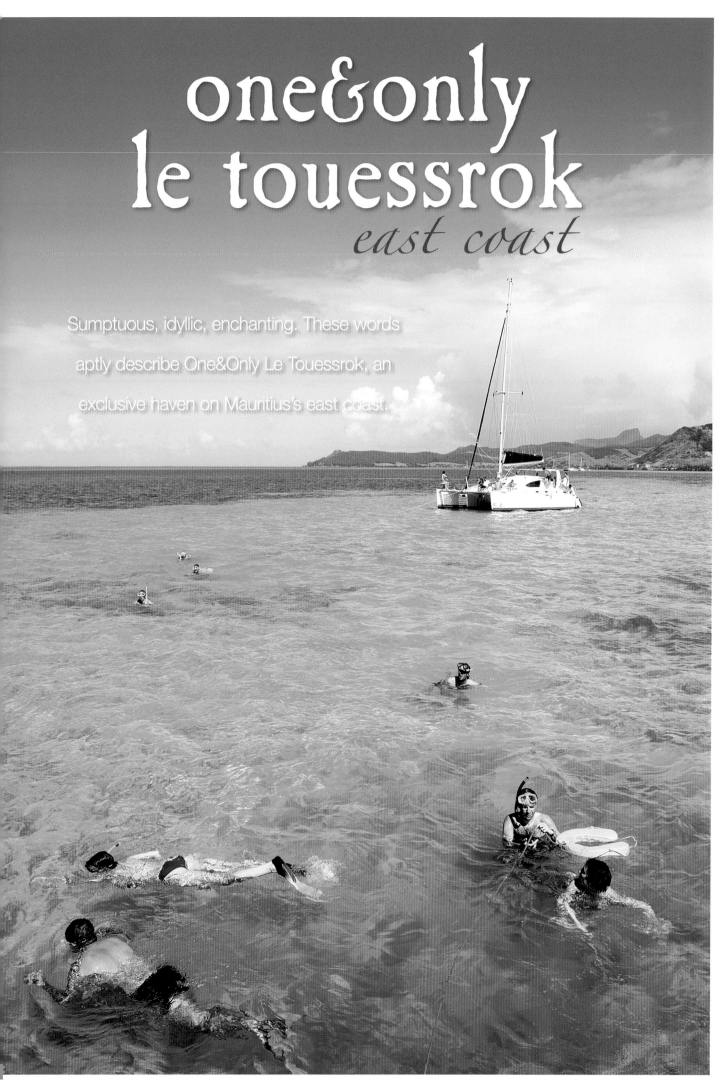

one&only
le touessrok
east coast

Sumptuous, idyllic, enchanting. These words

aptly describe One&Only Le Touessrok, an

exclusive haven on Mauritius's east coast.

I float over purple and pink anemones, sea slugs and hundreds of tiny fish that dart around me inquisitively

Beautiful bays and sandy white coves twist around the tropical peninsula. Wooden bridges span swimming pools and flowing waterways. Tanned residents laze on recliners under thatched umbrellas, holding fruity cocktails. Coconut palms fringe the beach where a honeymoon couple, ensconced in their romantic bliss, wade slowly into the clear water.

This is languid One&Only Le Touessrok, a tranquil slice of paradise on the east coast of Mauritius. The resort consists of six beaches, three separate islands, 200 suites and three private villas. It's just a short boat-ride away from spectacular Ile aux Cerfs, where a multitude of watersports awaits the active holidaymaker, and peaceful Ilot Mangénie, the resort's private, tranquil island.

The sun breaks through the clouds as I'm shown to my suite where my butler, Sada, greets me. 'Anything you need, please call me, any time,' he says flashing a broad Mauritian smile. The resort's several levels of accommodation are all sea-facing, with colourful Mauritian artwork and big bay windows. The Ocean Suites are perfect for families, and the Villas boast a level

of luxury fit for royalty, with state-of-the-art entertainment and communication systems.

I've had a tiring few days so, after unpacking, I head for the Givenchy Spa (all the therapists are Givenchy-trained) and a Swedish massage. The fragrant aroma of frangipani wafts through the airy corridors as I'm led to a treatment room. 'I'll be using almond oil, which is very good for sore muscles,' says Vanisha, my Mauritian masseuse. My body, stiff after a spell of waterskiing, first resists and then melts under her fingers. An hour later I drift out into the humid heat feeling calm and light-headed.

There's also plenty to keep sportsmen occupied. The free shuttle-boat ride to Ile aux Cerfs will reveal a playground of kayaks, sailing dinghies, Hobie cats, glass-bottomed boats, snorkelling, water-skiing and windsurfing. If you're prepared to spend a little extra, you can go scuba-diving, deep-sea fishing, parasailing or skim across the ocean on a catamaran.

Golf enthusiasts can play the 18-hole championship course designed by golfing star Bernhard Langer. Other sports include horseriding, hiking, cycling, volleyball and tennis.

Later, I head for dinner. There are seven restaurants, and I opt for Three Nine Eight, spread over three levels and specialising in cuisine from nine countries. The Creole buffet is delicious, particularly the mild chicken curry, with flambéed bananas for dessert.

I'm up before dawn the next day and wander down to the beach for another aqua experience, beginning with a catamaran cruise. A brilliant rainbow arcs over the ocean as *Vitamin Sea* sails across the bright blue water. The sun bakes down, turning the fair-skinned European guests a deep shade of red. After visiting a waterfall, we motor on to a shallow coral reef to snorkel. I float over purple and pink anemones, sea slugs and hundreds of tiny fish that dart around me inquisitively. While we snorkel, the crew prepares salads, chicken kebabs and dorado grilled in garlic for lunch.

Next stop is Ile aux Cerfs for a parasail over the ocean. The view is dramatic as I cruise high above the turquoise waters. Sun-drenched and pleasantly tired, I return to the resort as the sun sets in a blaze of golden colours.

PREVIOUS SPREAD Icons of the tropics, coconut palms dominate the gardens at One&Only Le Touessrok.

While guests investigate the rich marine life, crew on board prepare their lunch.

THIS SPREAD The golf course was designed by Bernhard Langer.

There are six inviting beaches.

The Givenchy Spa, where the cares of the world disappear beneath the fingers of Givenchy-trained therapists.

Accommodation is roomy and elegant.

The beaches are linked by wooden bridges.

details

When to go
Mauritius is a year-round destination. The wettest months
are from December to March, when occasional cyclones
may occur.

How to get there
World Leisure Holidays exclusively represents One&Only
Le Touessrok, and will arrange flights, transfers, accommodation
and excursions.

Who to contact
Tel. (0860) 95 4954 or go to *www.wlh.co.za*

garden of eden
seychelles

ANDREW WOODBURN

A serene, unspoilt beach on Cousine Island.

Scattered across the western Indian Ocean like a handful of gems is the Seychelles Archipelago. The more populated main islands lie south of the equator. To the north, far-flung atolls rise from clear aquamarine waters that are home to a wonderland of rainbow-coloured marine life. Resorts in this area range from the simple to the splendid; all, however, are passionate about the wonders their island homes have to offer.

INDIAN OCEAN

●denis

lémuria●
cousine● PRASLIN

CENTRAL SEYCHELLES

victoria■ ●cerf

kenya

MAHÉ

tanzania

seychelles

banyan tree●

←desroches

mozambique

madagascar
mauritius

banyan tree
mahé island

Focused on recreating the romantic atmosphere he and his wife

had experienced during their early travels, Singaporean Ho Kwon

Ping has created a chain of luxury resorts that ooze with seduction

and peace ... and a respect for the environment.

The banyan *Ficus benghalensis* is a hardy tree, but the aerial roots that grow down from its branches give it a certain balletic grace. The tree so impressed Singaporean businessman Ho Kwon Ping and his wife Claire Chiang that they named a hotel chain after it, and the Banyan Tree group has now spread its branches to Bahrain, Maldives, China, Seychelles and elsewhere. All offer seductive Eastern style, which the owners describe as providing 'sanctuary for the senses'.

The Seychelles Banyan Tree was built in 2002 on the south-west coast of Mahé Island at Intendance Bay, where a secluded beach curls beneath slopes covered with forests and a tumble of granite boulders. The hotel has been decorated in the style of a colonial plantation mansion, and has 60 private villas spread throughout the forest and on the beach.

My beach villa had its own horizon pool, spa pool and outdoor pavilion and was just a hop from the sands. State-of-the-art personal entertainment equipment incorporated a wide-screen TV, a DVD player and a music centre, complete with CD compilations of mystical sounds especially recorded for the Banyan group. The air was infused with the fragrance of jasmine, and each day brought new aromas – amber, citronella and the lemony extract of *Litsea cubeba*.

The open areas are at the centre of the resort. There's a breathtaking pool, a library, a shop selling Banyan Tree products and three restaurants. Saffron Restaurant, open in the evenings only, is suffused in a warm orange light and offers a menu of exquisitely prepared Thai and south-east Asian dishes. Breakfasts, lunches and dinners are served at Au Jardin d'Epices, and Chez Lamar's cuisine highlights Creole cuisine.

Yoga, mountain biking, horseriding, scuba-diving and tours to the island's capital, Victoria, as well as private beach picnics are on offer. However, the Banyan Tree group is known mostly for its spas, which have won a brace of international awards from readers of the US-based travel magazine *Condé Nast Traveler*. To reach the eight entirely private treatment pavilions, guests follow paths that wind between palms and granite outcrops. The design of the pavilions is, I was told, based on ancient traditions that date back centuries. The treatment techniques also have their roots in the past, and are 'low on technology and high on touch', such as stress-dissolving massages and body scrubs. The spa's signature treatment is the Royal Banyan, a three-hour session that includes an oil-free Thai acupressure massage followed by an application of herbal pouches moistened with warmed sesame oil. The oil is then used for a massage like that used to soothe the aches and pains of Thai royalty for centuries.

Banyan Tree's conservation initiatives are also soothing to the senses. I left the hotel with a small green turtle hand-made of cloth, which had been left on my bed as a token from the Green Imperative Fund. Optional donations made by guests (plus the same amount from the hotel) are channelled via the fund to local conservation programmes.

PREVIOUS SPREAD Surrounded by palms, the Banyan Tree's main building overlooks the 800-metre-long beach on Intendance Bay.

THIS SPREAD The beachfront Spa Pool Villa, just 10 steps from the sand.

The Presidential Villa has a free-form swimming pool built within the granite rocks.

A soothing herbal massage at the spa.

Five-star cuisine in a tropical setting.

The Banyan Tree's main swimming pool.

details

When to go
Seychelles is situated outside the cyclone belt and has warm weather all year. The rainy season is between December and February.

How to get there
The hotel is a 30-minute drive or five minutes by helicopter from Mahé International Airport.

Who to contact
Tel. (+248) 38 3500/38 3555, e-mail *seychelles@banyantree.com* or visit *www.banyantree.com*

cerf island resort

cerf island

Tucked into the voluptuous subtropical vegetation of Cerf Island
is a resort that is so indulgent you'll never want to leave.

It was early evening on the beach at Cerf Island resort in the Seychelles. I sat at a table with the sea on one side and a roaring fire on the other, watching the twinkling lights on distant Mahé Island. The chef had arranged a private beach dinner with French wine and crayfish, and the mood was just perfect. Then, after dinner, local entertainer David Scholastique arrived on the beach, guitar in hand, and, as night fell, the balmy velvet air was infused with the haunting lyrics of a French love song.

I had arrived on Cerf the previous day by boat from Mahé's Victoria Harbour. The narrow strait between these islands provided anchorage for pirates until 1756, when the French frigate *Le Cerf* arrived. On board was expedition leader Corneille Morphey, who claimed the island for France by laying a stone of possession on Mahé (the stone is now on display in the National Museum in Victoria). After the Napoleonic Wars, the British controlled the Seychelles until the 1970s, when it became independent.

Cerf is part of the so-called 'Inner Islands', an archipelago of 42 islets that were formed some 120 million years ago when Madagascar and India split from the African continent. The island is roughly circular and small, about one kilometre in diameter.

Cerf Island Resort stands on steeply sloping ground in a jumble of granite, ferns and forest, and has three Hideaway villas, four Hillside villas and five Tortoise

*The chef had arranged a private beach dinner with
French wine and crayfish, and the mood was just perfect*

suites. Paths connect the rooms to the horizon pool, spa and the 1756 Restaurant, with its 180-degree views of the ocean. All the villas have Creole names of local trees and creatures, such as Vyey Babonn (a coral-reef fish), Kakatwa (parrot), and Zourit (octopus), and are generously sized with satellite television, digital entertainment and ultra-modern bathrooms.

The hill above the resort affords glorious views of the islands (local pilots who use the chopper pad here say the view is the best in the archipelago) and is a popular spot to say 'I do'. Going for a flip is one of the most thrilling ways to see the islands, but the hotel also has kayaks and pedallos. Alternatively, trips in a glass-bottomed boat and fishing charters can be arranged.

Cerf is at the entrance to the Sainte Anne Marine National Park. No fishing is permitted in these waters, but their shallowness ensures excellent snorkelling. Just a few metres from the beach at the resort we were surrounded by thousands of striped sergeant majors.

Neighbouring Moyenne belongs to Brendan Grimshaw, a colourful Yorkshire newspaperman who has spent the past 30 years on his island, which is home to giant Aldabra tortoises and thousands of birds. The island has a museum, a little church and the Jolly Roger Restaurant, but the greatest attraction is spending time with this modern-day castaway. You can read all about his life and experiences in *A Grain of Sand*, a fantastical tale of black magic, encounters with sharks and a quest for buried pirate treasure.

Cerf Island Resort is mostly about romance and it does it well. Its full package, which culminates in a beach dinner, includes a hot-stone treatment in the spa and a romantic sunset cruise.

PREVIOUS SPREAD Swimming in the bar-side pool.

A rainbow world awaits snorkellers at the Sainte Anne Marine National Park.

THIS SPREAD A romantic dinner on the beach.

Tropical vegetation ensures privacy for guests who enjoy a spa bath.

The suites are furnished with a pleasing combination of casual island style and sophisticated European touches.

You could lose yourself in the views.

The cuisine focuses on the freshest harvest from the sea – naturally.

details

When to go
The resort is open all year.

How to get there
The island is a 20-minute transfer by boat (or five minutes by helicopter) from Mahé.

Who to contact
Tel. (+248) 29 4500, fax (+248) 29 4511, e-mail *info@cerf-resort.com* or go to *www.cerf-resort.com*

constance

lémuria resort
praslin

With all the beauty of the Garden of Eden, Praslin and its

five-star resort guarantee an island getaway second to none.

Kicking off my shoes, I plunged onto the magical beach tucked between giant boulders

PREVIOUS SPREAD The veranda overlooks a tranquil bay and a forest-swathed peninsula.

THIS SPREAD At Lémuria, the baths are big and the views are bigger.

The swimming pool has three levels, flowing from the main building to the sea.

The undulating golf course was designed by Marc Farry.

A junior suite. The resort has been constructed of local, natural materials.

The kilometre-long Grande Anse Kerlan.

When General Charles Gordon, of Khartoum fame, visited the Seychelles in 1881, he was convinced that the beautiful Vallée de Mai on Praslin was the site of the biblical Garden of Eden. He maintained that the Seychelles archipelago was once a part of a magical continent, Lémuria, which joined India to the island of Madagascar.

Driving into the Constance Lémuria Resort through lush vegetation, I felt that I, too, had entered an untouched part of paradise. We reached the top of a granitic hill, and I walked through huge doors to encounter the beaming, welcoming smiles of the Lémuria Seychellois reception staff. Around me, the foyer was cathedral-like in volume, with massive wooden beams and high ceilings, drawing the eye first upwards and then out to the magnificent view beyond.

Lémuria Resort's main building lies on the slopes of a hill and is made from local wood and stone, which blend perfectly with the natural surroundings. The swimming pool has three levels, flowing from the building to the sea. This five-star destination has 96 suites (88 junior and eight senior), eight villas and one presidential villa. The suites lie scattered along two pristine beaches, one to the south-west and the other facing north-west. Each suite is positioned just 15 metres from the beach, inviting you to pull on your swimming costume and head for the water. The south-west beach, Grande Anse Kerlan, is a kilometre-long curve of soft white sand; that on the north-west, although smaller, is perfectly positioned to enjoy sunsets with a delicious cocktail.

After exploring both beaches, I was determined to investigate what for me is Lémuria's real treasure. Hiring a motorised golf cart, I drove up and over the unique, undulating Marc Farry 18-hole international golf course to my destination, a hidden cove. Kicking off my shoes, I plunged onto the magical beach tucked between giant boulders – Anse Georgette. I tugged on my snorkel and goggles, and took to the water.

After a day of superb snorkelling, I decided to indulge myself at Le Spa de Constance, a world-class facility, where guests can unwind and enjoy a little, or a lot, of pampering. I selected a treatment called 'Seychellois Exotic Dream'. Later, with my muscles pummelled and coaxed into sleepy submission, I headed back to my suite.

The Seychellois are connoisseurs of the good things that the Indian Ocean has to offer the palate. To savour some of this abundance, I strolled to Lémuria's restaurant perched on boulders overlooking the ocean, and indulged in a festival of flavours – red snapper, bonito, lobsters and prawns. I let my mind drift lazily to General Gordon. He wasn't wrong; here on the Seychelles you certainly feel close to something extraordinary!

details

When to go
The resort is open all year.

How to get there
Praslin is 15 minutes from Mahé by air and one hour on the *Cat Cocos* catamaran ferry.

Who to contact
Tel. (+248) 28 1281, e-mail *resa@lemuriaresort.com* or go to *www.lemuriaresort.com* or *www.constance-hotels.com*

cousine island

cousine island

Tranquillity, unspoilt birdlife and pristine beaches marked only by
the flippers of turtles emerging from the warm sea to lay their eggs –
this is the archetypal tropical island paradise.

The transfer to Cousine Island was a real treat. Having been met at the airport on Praslin Island by a representative from Helicopter Seychelles, I was whisked away from the crowds to my own Bell Jet Ranger, which was standing by for the 15-minute flight due west of the main island.

On our approach, we hovered above the island like a bird, and gazed down upon this 25-hectare emerald isle, one of the Seychelles' Inner Islands. Tropical vegetation smothered its surface, rimmed by powdery white beaches and circled by large, reddish granitic outcrops rising out of the ocean.

Island manager Jock Henwood and his team were waiting for me as we landed. We hopped onto a golf cart and headed through the forest to the resort. The trees were alive with birds, and we had to make an unscheduled stop to give way to a huge Aldabra tortoise that was feeding on the path. The island's motto is: 'Where nature thrives and man is a silent observer', Jock explained. Cousine is the only island in the archipelago that is totally free of alien animals.

We pulled up at the resort, and I was shown to my huge luxury beachfront villa, decorated in French colonial style. There are only four villas on Cousine, each completely private, with a veranda, Jacuzzi, kitchenette and mini bar. There's a dining room, bar, lounge and well-stocked library for general use, but, as guests are limited to just four couples at a time, you're ensured tranquillity. This luxurious sanctuary of silence is the perfect spot to re-energise and relax. And peace of mind is assured – all profits from your stay are used to fund maintenance of the island's natural heritage.

In 1992, Cousine Island was purchased as a reserve, and a resort was established to fund a number of conservation projects, including one to protect the sea turtles that come to nest here each year, and another to protect the existing populations of five endemic birds. I spent an afternoon with a local conservation officer, who pointed out some of the island's specials, including the Seychelles magpie robin (one of the rarest landbirds), the Seychelles warbler and the Seychelles fody. Scrambling over huge granite boulders, we passed lesser noddy nests and fairy terns perched in almost every tree. We reached the island's highest point, and I was mesmerised by the sight of frigatebirds gliding by and white-tailed tropicbirds soaring and diving a few metres from me.

There is also a population of giant Aldabra tortoises, which were brought here from nearby islands. Between September and January, both green and hawksbill turtles scramble onto the beach to lay their eggs. The island's vegetation has been extensively rehabilitated – alien species have been eradicated and flora indigenous to the region has been reintroduced. Since 1995, more than 2 000 native trees have been planted.

I climbed onto an ancient boulder and gazed down at the sheer beauty below – island, forest and endless turquoise sea. I sighed at the magnificence of it all, and headed back to my luxury villa for a soothing shower and the fine island cuisine that awaited me.

PREVIOUS SPREAD A 25-hectare paradise, Cousine Island is a privately owned nature reserve.

THIS SPREAD The island is home to five species of endemic birds.

An old Aldabra tortoise. Males weigh an average of 250 kilograms.

Just four couples at a time may visit the lodge, and complete relaxation and attentive care is ensured.

The dining room and lounge overlook a sparkling pool.

The views will have you pondering all the synonyms for the word 'blue'.

The island's motto is:
'Where nature thrives and
man is a silent observer'

details

When to go
The resort is open all year.

How to get there
The island can be reached by helicopter from Mahé or Praslin.

Who to contact
Tel. (+248) 32 1107, e-mail *cousine@seychelles.net* or go to
www.cousineisland.com

denis
island

denis island

Rising from the sea like a gemstone, Denis Island offers the

finest hospitality in the most unspoilt natural environment.

As my aeroplane descended over crescent-shaped Denis Island, I noticed that it was ringed by an almost continuous, startlingly white beach. It was evident that the island was a coral cay, composed of the calcareous skeletons of millions of dead colonies of coral. Like many of the islands that lie on the northerly rim of the Seychelles Bank, Denis is a sandy, low-lying coral atoll covered in palm trees, and it rose like a jade jewel from the sparkling turquoise water of the Indian Ocean.

The island was named L'Isle Denis by Denis de Trobriand, commander of the *Etoile*, who in 1773 claimed its possession in the name of King Louis XVI of France. I was told by one of the local inhabitants that a number of treasures left by De Trobriand have yet to be found, including a bottle that contains the Act of Possession. But the natural treasures are everywhere – this 120-hectare island of untouched foliage, exotic flowers and idyllic beaches is valued by many visitors, especially the honeymoon couples who come to enjoy the tranquil privacy and beauty.

The island was purchased in 1999 by the Mason family, who have rebuilt and refurbished the private lodge that was erected in the 1970s. The new décor incorporates many local natural elements, such as driftwood, seashells and coral. My large spacious chalet was privately situated beneath coconut palms, with a sea-facing veranda and a private courtyard

This island of untouched foliage, exotic flowers and idyllic beaches is valued by many visitors

PREVIOUS SPREAD Denis Island, on the northern fringes of the shallow Seychelles Bank, is an emerald-green paradise with white beaches and fish-filled coral reefs.

THIS SPREAD The fragrant frangipani.

Crescent-shaped, the island is just 120 hectares in size.

One of Air Seychelles' colourful fleet.

Chalets open directly on to the beach.

The communal rooms are designed to encourage guests to unwind in tropical style.

Giant tortoises, a tumble of exotic foliage and a maze of winding paths encourage exploration.

Soft lighting illuminates the evening lounge.

The waters are a magnet to big-game fishermen. Dog-tooth tuna, barracuda, sailfish and marlin are plentiful.

Denis Island lodge and its swimming pool at night.

A successful haul from the ocean.

with an open-air shower. It had air-conditioning and tea- and coffee-making facilities, a mini bar and an en-suite bathroom with a double vanity unit.

Outside, one of the island's renowned kilometre-long white beaches lay at my disposal, with a lounger on the sand that I vouched to return to later. There is also a TV and games room. The French and Creole cuisine is sea-based, as would be expected, but the lodge also has its own vegetable garden, as well as chickens, cows, ducks and rabbits.

Armed with mask, fins and snorkel, I went snorkelling at the house reef straight off the beach. The protected pristine waters did not disappoint; visibility was excellent and the diversity of fish took my breath away. The diving here is among the best in the Seychelles area, especially at the point where the Seychelles Bank plummets steeply to a depth of 2 000 metres, producing spectacular sea walls and abysses. Swimming, watersports and trips in a glass-bottomed boat are also available, as well as game fishing.

Strolls around the island's network of paths will reveal a village, its houses dating back to the 1930s (the inhabitants work mainly at the hotel or on its farm), a pretty chapel and an old lighthouse built in 1910 to warn ships of the shallows at the island's northerly perimeter. There's also a fascinating old cemetery and the remains of a redundant copra mill.

*The pristine waters did
not disappoint;
visibility was excellent
and the diversity of fish
took my breath away*

DAVID ROGERS

Later, after an evening of rum-based cocktails, a sensational seafood meal eaten to the accompaniment of a Creole band, and an earful of entertaining stories delivered by the resort's own 'old man of the sea', Rolly, I decided to join some honeymoon couples the following morning on a deep-sea fishing venture. We returned to a chef whose face became wreathed with smiles as he saw our catch of sailfish, yellowfin tuna, wahoo and dorado.

Regretfully, I packed to leave. Thumbing through the visitors' book, I chanced upon the comments written by previous guests: 'We slowed down our movements and speeded up our emotions. Our senses were awakened again. We smelled the perfumes of the sea and earth, we saw colours of great power, we tasted perfect flavours, we touched the spirit of men who believe ... in nature. Denis, please do not change.'

I couldn't have said it better.

The Seychelles is a haven for divers. The best months for calm, clear water are March to May, and October to December. Many dive sites have easy shore access.

No expense has been spared to ensure the comfort of the guests.

Dine in style beside the gently swishing water.

The bar encourages guests to while away an hour or two and share their island adventures.

We returned to a chef whose face became wreathed with smiles as he saw our catch of fish

details

When to go
The resort is open all year. December and January are the wettest months.

How to get there
The island is a 30-minute trip by air from Mahé Island.

Who to contact
Tel. (+248) 32 1143 or e-mail *denisfo@ seychelles.net*

ANDREW WOODBURN

desroches
island resort

desroches island

The idyllic resort on the main island in the Amirantes archipelago

is a portal to a tropical palette of snow-white beaches, emerald

vegetation, shimmering water and a rainbow of fish.

It is January. White cumulus clouds balloon above the turquoise-blue Indian Ocean, and it is hot. Armed with a hat, a pair of shorts and a sarong, I set off to explore the 14 kilometres of white sandy beaches that fringe the Seychelles' Desroches Island. Regular markings on the sand indicate that loggerhead and leatherhead turtles have visited in the night to lay their eggs. Now, in the heat of the day, all is quiet except for ghost crabs scuttling busily up the beach, and the occasional splash of young stingrays and white-tipped reef sharks hunting in the shallow lagoons.

Desroches and its wild beaches lie some 250 kilometres south-west of Mahé in the Seychelles's Amirantes archipelago. It is one of the 'Outer Islands' and one of 25 coral cays that form the archipelago. Amirantes means 'admiral' in Portuguese, and these 'islands of the admiral' were named for the navigator Vasco da Gama who was the first to chart the surrounding waters. Desroches itself bears the name of an 18th-century governor of

Mauritius, to the south, who sent sailors to investigate the economic potential of the archipelago.

Visitors like myself have a much easier time of it. By air, it takes less than an hour from Mahé to Desroches, and the strip ends virtually at the Desroches Island Resort. The retreat is run by Naïade Resorts, which manages exclusive resorts and spas in Mauritius, Seychelles and the Maldives.

Upon arrival, we sat in the lounge, sipped a cool coconut-milk drink and admired our spotlessly maintained surroundings. Gazing around, I saw a crystal-clear swimming pool, with a mosaic of a blue surgeonfish beckoning from its depths, poolside tables with crisp linen and gleaming cutlery, and immaculately dressed waiters poised with menus that promised a range of soups, fish dishes and delectable desserts.

The lodge's 20 villas, all connected by a long walkway, are invitingly air-conditioned. Each has a four-poster, king-sized bed, an en-suite bathroom, a satellite television, a bar fridge, and a private balcony that spills onto the beach.

I was thrilled to discover two bicycles – a 'his' and a 'hers' – which had been left outside our front door to encourage visitors to explore the island. To make the journey hassle-free, a map had been provided that clearly indicated the network of paths and roads.

Our adventure had begun. We set off early one morning to explore sandy coves, the lighthouse, the copra village and the large enclosure where three giant tortoises seem comfortably at home. We also cycled past the only private house on the island, the exclusive resort of the President of the Seychelles.

Dive sites here are among the best in the world, with coral-capped reefs and steep drop-offs into blue and exciting caves. Angel Fish Dive Centre (a Professional Association of Diving Instructors-certified company) has a team here that took us to Canyons, which had exciting 'swim-throughs' and interesting coral crevasses populated by groupers, surgeonfish and innumerable goldies. In addition, there are sufficient other attractions to keep you happily occupied for a week, such as big-game fishing, exploring and any of the myriad treatments offered at the Coconut Spa.

PREVIOUS SPREAD Divers at the island's coral reefs will discover a kaleidoscope of fishes and other marine life.

Southern Desroches Island from the air.

THIS SPREAD Beautiful Madame Zabre beach, a tree-backed slope of soft white sand.

Le Veloutier restaurant overlooks the resort's swimming pool.

Deep-sea fishermen are attracted to the region's rich stocks of tuna and marlin.

Cycling is the best way to explore the island's inland treasures.

The décor is a fusion of island style and Mediterranean chic.

DESROCHES

DESROCHES

details

When to go
The resort is open all year.

How to get there
Desroches Island is reached via a 40-minute flight from Mahé.

Who to contact
Tel. (+248) 22 9003, fax (+248) 22 9002, e-mail
desroche@seychelles.net or go to *www.naiaderesorts.com*

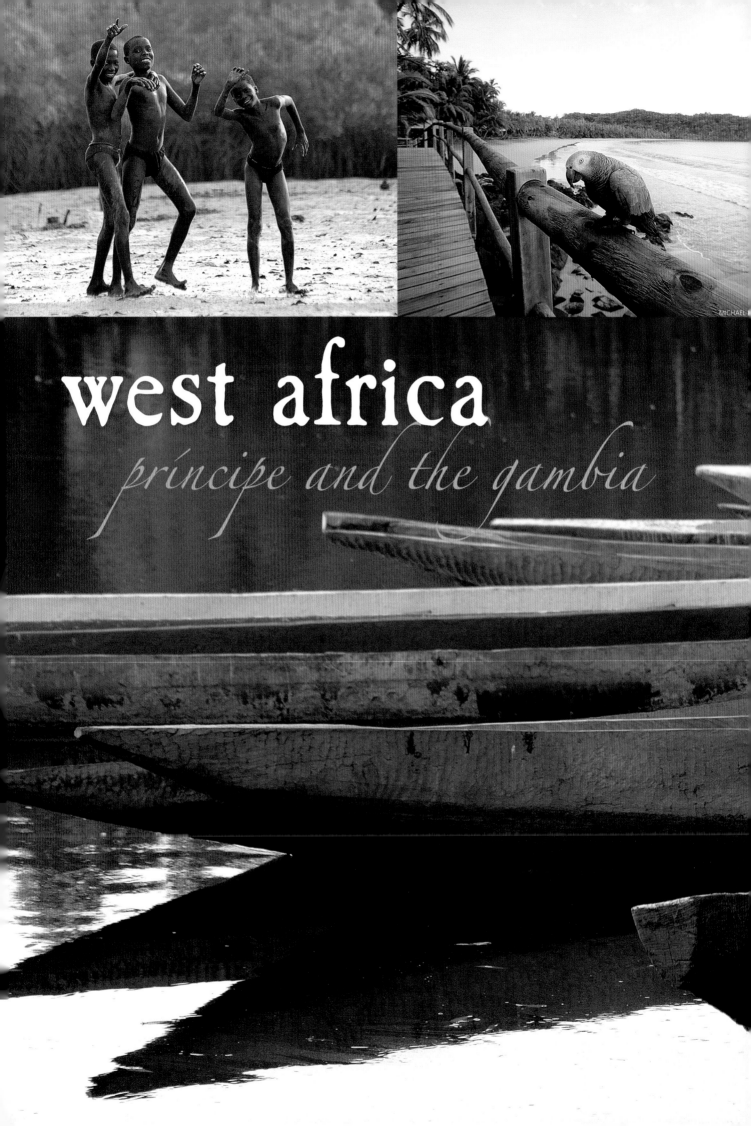

west africa

príncipe and the gambia

MICHAEL POLIZA

The islands and waterways of West Africa are on the up-and-up in the tourism stakes. Príncipe Island, part of the Democratic Republic of São Tomé and Príncipe, is small in size but big in beauty. There are forests, mountain peaks, magnificent wildlife, a luxury lodge and all that ocean. To the north-west, near the Gambia River's exit to the Atlantic Ocean, is a tranquil forest retreat that is a tribute to the passion and eco-awareness of its owners.

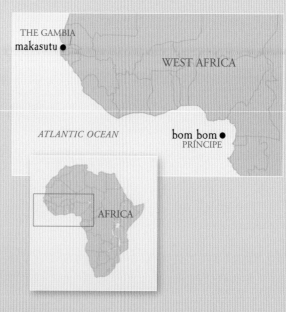

THE GAMBIA
makasutu ●

WEST AFRICA

ATLANTIC OCEAN

bom bom ●
PRÍNCIPE

AFRICA

Fishing boats on the Gambia River.
MARK EVELEIGH (3)

bom bom

island resort

príncipe

This resort is situated on a remote tropical island in the Gulf of Guinea, off West Central Africa, with bird-filled rainforests, crystal-clear waterfalls, pristine beaches and friendly people.

Holding a cooling drink in a coconut cup, I survey the beach from the veranda of my bungalow. This is my home for the next few days – Bom Bom Island Resort. Its two sections, the 21 bungalows, a duty-free shop and a swimming pool on Príncipe, and a restaurant and bar on smaller Bom Bom Island, are linked by a wooden footbridge that spans a 230-metre channel of aquamarine water.

Following a superb lunch – I am unable to resist the freshly caught barracuda – I set off for Santo Antonio, the capital town. Embraced by mountains and sea, it is bustling and colourful, with old colonial buildings and friendly people. The atmosphere is warm, safe and welcoming. Evening falls sooner than I would have liked, and I head back to Bom Bom. At Bar Pescador, I am given a cocktail by a smiling barman. Taking it onto the deck, I watch the moon rise over the Atlantic, and it slowly dawns on me that I am in paradise.

Dinner is served on the restaurant's wooden deck, accompanied by fine wines from South Africa. The Indian chef is only too pleased to share his knowledge with me. He produces dish after dish of wonderful cuisine, and I sample them all, with satisfied 'oohs' and 'aahs'.

The next morning, I am awoken by Chaplin, the resort parrot, squawking: '*Knock, knock, tring-tring, bom dia, bom dia.*' I breakfast on local fruits and freshly squeezed pineapple juice, then mount a quad-bike and follow Ramos, my guide, into the jungle. On the way, he shares his knowledge of the local fauna and flora. We arrive at the cliffs of Belo Monte, where a 60-metre abseil has been set up. Holding my breath, I ease myself over the edge and almost immediately encounter a colony of swallow nests. Beneath me is Praia Banana beach and, as I land on the silky, soft sand, the adrenalin is rushing through my veins. Smiling at my excitement, Ramos produces a picnic with fresh fruit, fish and freshly picked coconuts. After lunch, we set off to explore the massive volcanic boulders just below the waterline, then return to Bom Bom in kayaks, visiting a local fishing village on the way. I spend the evening enjoying a beach barbecue and listening to a local Príncipean band.

I awake at dawn the next morning. A driver-guide, Ti, has agreed to show me the old plantations, or *roças*, established largely by Portuguese landlords around the turn of the 20th century. As we drive around the island, it becomes evident why Príncipe was the world's largest producer of cocoa in the late 1900s. Spectacular buildings, once the homes of wealthy plantation owners, have now fallen into disrepair. We receive a warm welcome from the poor, but friendly islanders who make

PREVIOUS SPREAD A 230-metre walkway connects Príncipe to Bom Bom Island.

THIS SPREAD Soft lighting, swaying palms and a gently sloping beach – Bom Bom is a haven of peace.

Bird-filled tropical forest embraces the resort.

The entire population of the islands is of immigrant descent.

Fine South African wines complement the excellent cuisine.

I watch the moon rise over the Atlantic, and it slowly dawns on me that I am in paradise

BOM BOM ISLAND RESORT

a living on these once-gracious *roças*. We drive through the fishing village of Praia Abade, where I spend some time watching local fishermen building a dugout canoe. Hundreds of dried flying fish lie neatly arranged among the fishing huts that line the beach.

The following day, I explore the natural beauties of the eastern coast of Príncipe with a guide. We drive past Jocky's Cap, a 305-metre rocky outcrop rising from the sea that is home to dozens of the aptly named Príncipe paradise birds. We then sail to Rio São Tomé, spotting on the way two hump-backed whales that make me grab my camera as they breach and lob their tails, We disembark at Praia Akara for a short walk through the jungle to Rio São Tomé. The views of mountain pinnacles and cliffs are breathtaking. Feeling hot, I plunge into a rock pool, and am serenaded by African grey parrots in the trees. Ramos throws small pieces of coconut into the river, and attracts a catch of freshwater shrimps. Barbecued with a little salt and lemon juice, they are melt-in-the-mouth sublime.

After lunch, we continue into the jungle. We seem to encounter wonders behind almost ever tree – volcanic boulders, extraordinary flora and lianas, and brightly coloured birds that come to investigate the intruders.

We continue our circumnavigation up the west coast. Argentino, the captain, orders the fishing lines cast, and within minutes a strike makes the rod zing. I jump into the fishing chair and soon the largest wahoo I have ever seen is lying on the deck. That evening, dinner is on me! This is a fisherman's paradise, and fish like blue marlin, sailfish, dorado and kingfish are commonplace.

By the time the wahoo reaches my plate, it has been turned into *molho de fogo*, a fabulous traditional meal served with breadfruit, bananas, salads and some *malagueta*, an extremely hot peri-peri sauce, to give it a kick.

The following morning I pack my bags and, sadly, say farewell to the friendly staff. As the plane takes off, I look down on Bom Bom with its sparkling waters and beautiful reefs. I'll return one day. Hopefully, it will be soon.

MICHAEL POLIZA

I plunge into a rock pool, and am serenaded by African grey parrots in the trees

Friendly and accommodating staff ensure that every guest has a wonderful holiday experience.

Exploring the extraordinary rocky outcrops and vegetated islands. Príncipe has seven endemic bird species.

Reed-roofed decks, rustling palms and beautiful views entice visitors to Bom Bom to kick back and relax.

The forest-lined beaches are pristine.

BOM BOM ISLAND RESORT (3)

details

When to go
Bom Bom Resort is open all year. Temperatures are consistently high; the rains fall between October and November, and from March to May. It is dry from December to February, and from June to September.

How to get there
There are flights to Príncipe (via São Tomé) from Lisbon, Gabon, Cameroon and Nigeria. Transport from the airport is included in the booking fee.

Who to contact
Tel. (+31-26) 370 5567, e-mail *petra.zwart@operation-loango.com* or *reservations@operation-loango.com*, or go to *www.bom-bom.com* or *www.operation-loango.com*

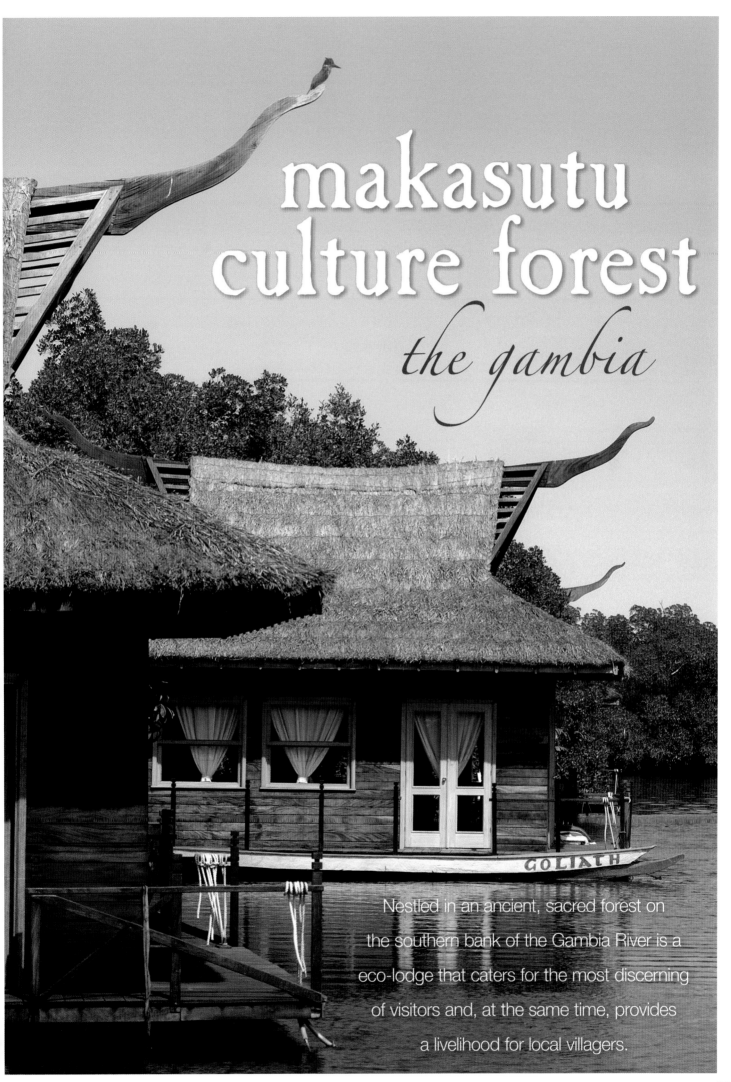

makasutu
culture forest
the gambia

Nestled in an ancient, sacred forest on
the southern bank of the Gambia River is a
eco-lodge that caters for the most discerning
of visitors and, at the same time, provides
a livelihood for local villagers.

such an important part of the Gambian psyche. The Muslims had long ago made the forest a place of prayer: literally a Mecca (Maka) in the forest (sutu), and it was seen as a sacrilege to fell trees or hunt here. Unaffected by the spirits, Lawrence and his friend James English spent several years living in a basic camp while they worked to get their project off the ground.

Slowly the locals began venturing close to the forest, and one day Lawrence and James discovered that a large section of trees had been felled beside their boundary fence. Fearing the forest's disappearance, the Englishmen raised the money to buy the land outright, and over the next few years replanted no fewer than 20 000 trees.

Finding alternative employment for the local community became a major concern, and so began the drive to create something more than a humble backpacker camp. Now, 15 years later, a workforce of more than 250 locals work at Mandina River Lodge and at nearby Makasutu Cultural Village, designed to bring the Gambian culture to the notice of tourists. Fresh produce is bought daily from the surrounding farmers and 99 per cent of the building materials have been sourced locally. As many as 3 500 people are indirectly benefited by the growth of tourism in the area.

Makasutu is now The Gambia's number-one ecotourism initiative. The British Guild of Travel Writers has awarded it 'Best Overseas Development' and the UK's *Sunday Times* has dubbed Makasutu's Mandina River Lodge 'The Best New Eco Hotel in the World.'

The lodge's complex of houseboats and bungalows is certainly in a class of its own. The houseboats, with their private pontoon breakfast areas and magnificent four-poster beds, are among the finest in Africa. Under the eye of your own boatman-guide, peaceful evening paddles along Mandina Bolong (channel) will reveal monkeys, baboons, manatee, crocodiles and an estimated 550 species of Gambian birds.

James and Lawrence are now working to unite a dozen local chiefs behind the Ballabu Conservation Project, an 85-square-kilometre conservation area on the Gambia River. Each village will be provided with its own community projects (such as eco-lodges) and individual wildlife parks that will attract tourists. All profits will go to education, healthcare, water and agricultural aid. 'There's really no limit to Gambian potential,' says James. 'I can foresee a time when The Gambia could become a travel hub for this fascinating part of West Africa.'

TEXT AND PHOTOGRAPHS BY MARK EVELEIGH

I wake at dawn and open the curtains of my houseboat onto a sunlit stretch of the Gambia River. I wander out to sit on my private pontoon, and order a hearty breakfast from my personal waitress. My private boatman-guide Buba arrives to plan a morning safari down the creek to watch monkeys and to look for the big crocodile that we'd seen the evening before. The waves lap against the pontoon, rocking me gently as a large monitor lizard slithers up onto the little bridge that connects my houseboat with the rest of the world. I can only assume that he too is part of the staff – my own private monitor lizard. It's hard to keep your feet on solid ground when you're living on a houseboat at one of Africa's finest eco-lodges.

Back in 1992, two English adventurers arrived in The Gambia, searching for a location on which to build a backpacker camp. They found the perfect spot in a 1.6-hectare section of Makasutu Forest. 'There are demons here, apparently,' Lawrence Williams explains. 'It's what has kept the place relatively untouched.' These creatures straddle the cultural mix of Islam and animism that is

PREVIOUS SPREAD Mandina River Lodge's four solar-powered suites and one stilted house offer panoramic views of the Mandina Bolong, a tributary of the Gambia River.

THIS SPREAD The holy man at Makasutu Cultural Village.

The floating houseboat lodges have been furnished in sophisticated style.

Each lodge has its own boatman-guide in attendance.

Exploring the mangroves that line the river.

At night, all that can be heard is the swish of the river and the sounds of the bush.

details

When to go
Makasutu Culture Forest and Mandina River Lodge are open
all year.

How to get there
Makasutu Forest and Mandina River Lodge are a 20-minute drive
from Banjul International Airport. Lodge transfers can be arranged.

Who to contact
E-mail *info@makasutu.com* or go to *www.makasutu.com* or
www.gambia.co.uk

travel advice

ORGANISING YOUR TRIP

While you can plan an island escape to most of the resorts and lodges featured by contacting them directly, it is often simpler to employ the services of a specialist tour operator to coordinate your visit. In selecting your destinations and accommodation, you'll need to specify your preferred type of holiday. Do you like a rustic lodge on the edge of a beach or do you want to be pampered at an exclusive spa resort? Are deep-sea fishing or diving on your list of dreams? Are you a dedicated birdwatcher or are you passionate about history and ancient cultures? An experienced operator will tailor-make an itinerary to accommodate both your scope of interests and your budget.

On pages 165–7 a list of experienced tour operators has been included for your convenience. All are equipped to help you arrange your dream vacation.

A traditional dhow.

Indian Ocean atoll, Zanzibar.

EAST AFRICAN ISLANDS

When to go
April and May are classified as the rainy season and many hotels and resorts are closed during this period. For the rest of the year, the weather is generally fine and warm. The best months for diving are from October to March when the wind is minimal and visibility is good. Mid-year is pleasant with low humidity, while the period between December and March is hot, sunny and humid.

Getting there
Several airlines, from both Africa and Europe, have regular flights to Dar es Salaam and Zanzibar in Tanzania and to three international airports in Kenya, including Nairobi. It's also possible to arrive by rail, road or ship. Visas may be required.

Money matters
Tanzania's unit of currency is the Tanzanian shilling; Kenya's is the Kenyan shilling. US dollars and euros are widely accepted, as are travellers' cheques, although at a slightly less favourable rate. Many hotels, travel agencies, safari companies and restaurants accept credit cards.

Medical matters
Malaria is prevalent throughout East Africa and its islands and precautions should be taken. Consult your doctor for the anti-malarial drugs that best suit your health and circumstances. A yellow fever vaccination is no longer officially required when entering Tanzania, but many doctors recommend one as a precaution.

Don't miss
Snorkelling around the islands' coral reefs with their multicoloured marine life; deep-sea fishing; sea turtles; whales between August and October; whale sharks and manta rays; varied birdlife; long, unpopulated beaches; a sunset sail on a dhow; mangrove forests; coconut and clove plantations.

MOZAMBIQUE

When to go
The best time to visit is during the dry, cooler winter months between April and September. Heavy rains often fall between January and March, making many roads impassable. Coastal resorts are very busy during the Christmas and Easter holiday periods, and advance bookings are advisable.

Getting there
Several airlines, including LAM, Air Portugal and Kenya Airways, fly directly into Maputo. South African Airways flies from Johannesburg to Maputo, while Pelican Air operates between Johannesburg and Vilanculos. Luxury buses operate between Maputo and neighbouring countries. Onward journeys can be arranged via the lodges. Visas may be required.

Money matters
Mozambique's local currency is the metical, but US dollars and the South African rand are accepted as payment in many places. It is advisable to carry cash or travellers' cheques, as credit cards are not widely accepted.

Medical matters
Visitors need a yellow fever vaccination certificate to enter Mozambique. Malaria is a problem throughout the country and the necessary precautions and preventative medication should be taken.

Don't miss
Deep-sea fishing in the Mozambique Channel; the lushly vegetated coral islands of the Quirimbas, with their mangrove swamps and rich birdlife; snorkelling the coral reefs; dhow trips; freshwater lakes with crocodiles on Benguerra Island; whale sharks and manta rays.

MADAGASCAR

When to go
The rainy season is between December and April, with cyclones occasionally occurring between January to March. A good time to visit is immediately after the rainy season, when the countryside is lush and green. In September and October, lemurs give birth, while birding is best from September to December. For watersports and diving, any time is good and turtles hatch throughout the year on Nosy Iranja.

Getting there
Air Madagascar operates in several African and European countries with regular flights to Antananarivo. SA Airlink flies directly from Johannesburg to Nosy Be. Visas are required by all visitors.

Cycling on Ile Sainte Marie.

Money matters
The local currency is the ariary. Euros and dollars are the favoured currency for exchange. Hotels and restaurants accept most major credit cards.

Medical matters
Malaria is prevalent and the necessary preventative measures should be taken. A vaccination certificate against yellow fever is required for travellers coming from an infected area.

Don't miss
Beautiful beaches; diving in the marine reserves; deep-sea fishing; cycling; wildlife, especially the endearing lemurs; boat trips around the *tsingys*.

MAURITIUS

When to go
Mauritius is considered to be an all-year destination. The wettest months are from December to March, when occasional cyclones may occur. The period between April and October is usually warm and dry.

Getting there
There are daily flights to Mauritius from South Africa and several European countries. A visa is not generally required if your stay is less than three months.

Money matters
The Mauritian currency is the rupee. US dollars and the euro are widely accepted. Credit cards are normally accepted by banks, hotels, restaurants and tourist shops.

Medical matters
Malaria is not a threat in Mauritius. An international vaccination certificate against yellow fever is needed if arriving from an infected area.

Don't miss
Beautiful beaches; coral reefs; watersports; deep-sea fishing; golf; well-appointed spas; dinner beneath the stars; the delicious *camarons*, or fresh-water prawns.

SEYCHELLES

When to go
Seychelles has a year-round tropical climate with an average monthly temperature of 27° to 32°C. Cool and dry trade winds blow from May to September. The wettest months are December and January. The best months for snorkelling and scuba diving are April to May and October to November.

Getting there
Air Seychelles flies to Mahé from Johannesburg, Nairobi, London and other European capitals. There are two flights a week from Johannesburg.

A visa is not required to visit Seychelles. Visitors need a valid passport, a return air ticket and proof of hotel reservation.

Money matters
Euros and US dollars can often be used for payment.

Medical matters
Malaria is not a problem in Seychelles. It is generally a safe destination.

Don't miss
Great dive sites; deep-sea fishing; magical beaches; Creole cuisine; water-sports galore; strolling along the network of paths on Denis Island.

WEST AFRICA (Príncipe and The Gambia)

When to go
In Príncipe, the dry and cool months are between June and September. The rest of the year is hot and humid. The best time to travel in The Gambia is from November to February. During the wet season from June to October, some of the roads are impassable. The peak tourist season lasts from October to April, which coincides with the arrival of visiting migratory birds.

Getting there
Visitors to Príncipe usually arrive by air from Libreville in Gabon. To get to The Gambia, several airlines serve Banjul International Airport. It's also possible to travel to Banjul by road from Dakar in Senegal, a journey of about six hours. Banjul receives several cruise ships a year. Visas are required; enquire at your nearest Gabon embassy for further details. Visitors from the UK and several other countries do not require visas to visit The Gambia. Others should acquire a visa from a Gambian embassy prior to travel.

Money matters
The local currency in Príncipe is the dobra; in The Gambia it is the dalasi. It is advisable to keep some foreign currency in cash, as opposed to travellers' cheques, which are difficult to exchange.

Medical matters
There is a risk of yellow fever infection in Príncipe, so vaccination is required before entering the country. Malaria is widespread, particularly in the rainy season from October to April. To visit The Gambia, a yellow fever vaccination is required for those arriving from infected areas. Anti-malaria medicine is strongly recommended, as the country is a high-risk area.

Don't miss
In The Gambia: listening to the forest from your houseboat at night; exploring the Gambia River and Makasutu Culture Forest. In Príncipe: incredible rock formations; long, unspoilt beaches; excellent birdlife.

Passing this gate birds are slowing down, Why don't you do the same

A respect for nature in Mauritius.

Paris
FRANCE
Lyons
Toulouse
Marseilles
THAILAND
Bangkok
Every day, the Indian Ocean
within easy reach.
SEYCHELLES
COMOROS
MAYOTTE
Nosy Be
MADAGASCAR
MAURITIUS
Mahajanga
Toamasina
Antananarivo
REUNION
SOUTH AFRICA
Johannesburg
www.air-austral.com
AIR AUSTRAL
THE FRENCH AIRLINE OF THE INDIAN OCEAN

AFRICA
Geographic

An Africa Geographic publication
Africa Geographic
1st floor, Devonshire Court
20 Devonshire Road, Wynberg 7800
Cape Town, South Africa
www.africageographic.com

Reg. no. 1992/005883/07

First published 2007

Text & photographs © David Rogers, Jeremy Jowell and Ian Johnson
(with the exception of photographs individually credited)
Cover photograph of Seychelles © Martin Harvey

Editor Judy Beyer
Art director Bryony Branch
Project manager Jenni Saunders
Travel coordinator Janine Bellis

Reproduction in Cape Town by Resolution Colour (Pty) Ltd
Printed & bound by Tien Wah Press (Pte) Ltd, Singapore

ISBN 0 620 38178 9

AFRICA GEOGRAPHIC TRAVEL

Further information on all the establishments featured in *African Islands in Style* can be
found at the end of each entry. Your local travel agent or consultant should also be able to
provide help and advice. In addition, you are welcome to contact us at Africa Geographic Travel
– we would be delighted to help you plan a visit to these properties or any other destination in
Africa and its islands. Africa Geographic Travel offers many superb itineraries designed for the
readers of *Africa Geographic* magazine. More about these can be found on our website.
To order any titles in the *Safari in Style* series, find out more about each property featured,
participate in future publications or book an island escape, visit *www.safariinstyle.co.za*

Africa Geographic Travel
Devonshire Court
20 Devonshire Road
Wynberg 7700
Cape Town, South Africa
Tel. (+27-21) 762 2180
Fax (+27-21) 762 2246
E-mail *info@africageographic.com*
Website *www.africageographic.com/expeditions*